AF254761

Bullard Road

Stories of the Land and People... Within 2 Miles of Our Farm

Kurt Bullard

Copyright © 2026 by Kurt Bullard

ISBN: 978-1-969615-04-7

All rights reserved.

No portion of this book may be reproduced in any form without written permission from the publisher or author, except as permitted by U.S. copyright law.

Published by As You Wish Publishing
www.asyouwishpublishing.com
connect@asyouwishpublishing.com

Disclaimer:

The views, thoughts, and opinions expressed in this publication are those of the author(s) and do not necessarily reflect the official policy or position of As You Wish Publishing. Any content provided by the author is of their opinion and is not intended to malign any religion, ethnic group, club, organization, company, individual, or anyone or anything.

As You Wish Publishing nor Kurt Bullard assumes responsibility or liability for any errors or omissions in the content of this book. All content is provided "as is," with no guarantees of completeness, accuracy, usefulness, or timeliness.

This book is dedicated to all of my ancestors. They endured tough times, droughts, the dust bowl years, immigrating from Germany and Canada, crop failures, and wars. My mother was advised not to have children, due to her illnesses. My grandfather, Roy Bullard, and father, Herman, both were granted agriculture exemptions to avoid WWI and WWII. I am keenly aware of my small statistical chance of being born. I am also dedicating this book to my family and future generations. Similar stories of neighbors and friends are present in every part of our country. Stories become memories. Thank you to everyone that has given me a story to remember.

Contents

Author's Note

History can be used as a rudder to guide our lives. If we acknowledge it and use it, history can steer us along our river of life. If we choose to ignore our history, we will bounce along the rocks, drifting from day to day without purpose or direction. This is my purpose of the telling of these stories. By reading these stories, I hope someone learns a life lesson and uses this gained knowledge to improve their own life or avoids a misstep.

Note to the Reader

The roadmap for this book will start at the geographic location of our farm and work south for the entirety of a two-mile radius and then pivot west, then north and finally east before returning to the farm for more stories. The stories of the people will be sprinkled in between the land stories, as my memory is activated. The included stories are from my memory, or recollections of stories that were told to me by others. By chance you are reading these attempts at history, and recall any particular story differently, I apologize. Any chronological timeline will be abandoned and in place, you will find random recollections. The only pattern will be the geography encircling the farm.

Introduction

My great grandfather, Philip Aurelius Bullard, bought 40 acres, 7 miles east of Main Street, Elkhart, Indiana, on November 19, 1891. He and his mother, Elizabeth, had immigrated from Magog, Quebec, Canada years earlier. The only structure on the property was a log cabin located on the northeast corner of the 40 acres and set back about 100 feet from the two-lane, dirt road, now known as Middlebury Street. During that time, that stretch was commonly referred to as 'Bullard Road' because our homestead was the last one on that road. Philip had also petitioned the County to build the road. The roads to the north, east, and south from that point were only one-lane dirt trails. The stories surrounding 'Bullard Road' follow.

'The Bullard mansion' (The caption on the back of this photograph) Bullard Road in the foreground Circa 1920

Bullard Farms 1966

Chapter One

THE FARM

The Log Cabin Picture...

My entire life I have heard stories about the 'log cabin'. Pictures of the cabin were never found in the family picture trove. In 1896 the farmhouse was built and the cabin's use was changed from being a residence to a barn/animal shelter. There is no record, verbal or written, of when the log cabin was torn down or dismantled. After my father, Herman, passed away in 2010, a picture surfaced again while sorting through family photos. I had seen that photo many times. The picture was taken on the south side of the farmhouse looking east, presumably by my grandmother. My grandfather, Roy Bullard, was standing by a 1920 Ford with wood spoked wheels and 4- or 5-year-old Herman was seated on the steps looking at the car in the east driveway.

I took a picture of the picture with my smart phone and proceeded to zoom in to see more details of the picture. The elusive log cabin appeared in the background. No one had seen the cabin for over 75 years. I got in my truck, drove to the farm, and showed Mom my discovery. I only wish my dad was alive to see the log cabin picture.

Roy and Herman 1920 Ford Log Cabin in the background

The Barn...

The main barn was built in 1898. My great grandfather used a new method of laminating sawn lumber together for the main beams. The barn building method at the time used the traditional hand-hewn beams. Loading hay in the barn 120 years later, the boys from Paulus farms were positive the barn could not be as old as I had claimed due to the construction. I replied, "I had pictures" to prove the date. Both the farmhouse and the barn had slate roofs. I am uncertain how my great grandfather and my great, great grandmother gathered enough resources to construct both the house and the barn. My great, great grandmother also built, a house at 1034 Middlebury Street where she lived. That house is at that address today.

The barn originally was built in the practical design for the time with a drive through the middle of the barn. This drive-through design made it possible for a horse-drawn wagon to pull through the center of the barn without backing up. There were hay mows on both sides to store loose hay. A hay sling would be laid on an empty wagon and loose hay was elevated onto the wagon by a horse-drawn hay loader in the field. When the loaded wagon arrived back to the barn, a rope from the hay trolley that was located along the peak of the barn was attached to the hay sling. The stack of hay would be pulled to the peak of the barn by horse power and could be moved along the track and then released onto the area that was selected for the placement of the loose hay load. The hay mow had several trap doors and hay chutes where the loose hay could be forked down to the animals below. A feed alley with mangers and handmade wooden stanchions was the main feeding area in the barn.

At approximately age 9, I became very interested in the game of basketball and the east haymow became a small court with a hoop attached to a barn door for a backboard. Stacked hay bales were placed at the edge of the mow to prevent a player from falling 8-10 feet to the floor below. A few years later Dad had a floor built between the two hay mows and Bullard full court barn ball was born. I painted a center jump circle and painted the lanes. For the next 40 years, storing hay in the barn was never discussed; Dad wanted us to play ball. Almost everyone in the county who played basketball, played in our barn.

The Eldridge boys; Brian, Brett, and Brad, the Hoffmans, Weirichs, Cowles, Shawn Kemp and too many to remember or name, all played in our barn. Brad and Brett Eldridge were close in age and very young when they started playing ball in our barn. When teams were picked, the two of them counted as one player and we were referred to them as the 'fleas'. It wasn't long before we counted them as two players and they had to guard each other. 3 on 3, or 4 on 4 were the best games and the winners stayed on the court for the next challengers. On Sunday afternoons we would play until dark. Dad installed lights in the barn to allow longer playing time. We would play before catching chickens, after catching chickens, after school, after sorting sweet corn, and pretty much whenever we had free time. Every part of the barn was ruled out-of-bounds except the floor, the net, the rim, and the backboard. As our skills evolved, a player would be allowed to jump on the east wall and dunk without being declared out-of-bounds. The floor-to-ceiling hay chute was left intact and it could be used as the perfect pick to allow a clear shot. The hay chute also protected the stairway. When Pat Hackett ran for Congress in Indiana's 2nd District, Beth and I invited Pat and Rita Kohler to our farm for dinner. During the tour of the farm, we shared basketball stories. I learned that Pat was a point guard for her high school team. Her eyes lit up when I explained to her that we had a full court in our barn. We climbed the steep steps to the court and soon three pointers were being shot and free throws were being made.

Dinner included fresh picked green beans, "309" sweet corn, and fresh caprese salad. Discussions ensued involving family, politics, and life. She thought our barn might be a good backdrop for a campaign commercial highlighting Indiana values, education, youth, and farm families. The ad was scheduled, produced and aired. The commercial can be found online and provided a great memory. Pat was the kindest, smartest, and most dedicated candidate between the two choices. Indiana and the country would be a much better place if she would have won. Her district had been severely gerrymandered to select the voters instead of the voters selecting the candidate. There are times when the best candidate loses but retains their integrity. Her campaign proved this statement.

The ball bouncing on our court's wooden floor is a sound I will remember forever and the full court in our barn is one of the handful of things I miss about Elkhart.

Bullard Court

The Chicken Houses #1, #2, #3...

Chicken house #1 was obviously the first one to be built on the farm in the early 1900s. When it was built, it was divided into several pens to enable chicks to grow into pullets and then laying hens on a constant rotation. This system provided a constant supply of meat and eggs. Catching chickens in Chicken House #1 was my first paid job. I was 5 years old. By this time, the chicken house was just used for raising fryers or roasters. The classification of the flock was assigned based on genetics and their final weight. Fryers weighed three to four pounds and roasters weighed four to six pounds. Our chicken catchers were assigned the task of either catching the chickens or carrying them to the truck. Dad invented this procedure and it allowed smaller, younger help to just catch and the older, stronger boys would carry the chickens to the truck.

The catchers caught 3 or 4 chickens and the carriers either carried 6,7, or 8 chickens depending on how many were placed in the crates on the truck. The weather and the size of the chickens would dictate the number in each crate. If it was hot, fewer chickens would be placed in the crates and conversely if it was cold, more chickens would be loaded in each crate. I was tasked with catching one and bringing it to the door where they were loading. Loading the trucks took place after dark and our only guidance through the maze of feeders and waterers were a few red light bulbs that replaced the normal light bulbs. The darkness calmed the chickens to allow for easy capture.

Dad got preliminary loan approval to build chicken house #2. The plan for the building was an ambitious 40' x 200' cement block building that could house 12,500 chickens, literally increasing our farm's capacity tenfold. A local crew was hired for the construction, the excavation was done and the fill dirt was placed in between the poured footers. That was when Dad got the news that the final approval for the loan was denied. The bank's excuse was that Dad did not own the land. He was an only child. He would inherit the farm. I am convinced the bank wanted to tie up the entire farm as collateral. That was probably their plan from day one. Dad moved ahead with the project as cash became available. My loathing of the banking industry started at this time and continues today.

I remember my enjoyment of riding my bike on the long cement floor for the short time between the end of construction and the first chicks arriving. One of Dad's many mantras included the saying; 'a sign of a growing farm or business is the pouring of concrete'. Housing chickens, storage, and shelter at the south end of the chicken house for a few cattle were the only uses of chicken house #2. It was a good 20–30-year run, and chicken house #3 was built in the late 60's. The structure of the original design was planned for the ability to add a second story. This was added a few years later.

The manure from the second story was shoveled down through trap doors in the floor. Dad and Bob Garver were the last two farmers in our area to own their own chickens. Vertical integration, low margins, and corporate manipulation of the supply chain all contributed to the elimination of farmer-owned poultry. At the end of our chicken enterprise the only benefit was the manure and providing enough net income to support the salary of our hired man. In the mid 70's the decision was made to stop raising chickens. We applied more commercial fertilizer to replace the manure. The risk of raising and marketing chickens was also eliminated.

Chicken House #2

Farmstead growth...

The farmstead grew from a lone log cabin in 1891 to the last of the 15 buildings being built in 1974. One of our farm buildings was a double ear-corn crib that housed an elevator. Dad followed a Purdue University blueprint to construct the corn crib in 1948. A saw mill was set up close to our woods to cut the lumber needed for the construction.

In the late 40's, the industry was on a fast track switching from ear corn to shelled corn storage. Dad said the double crib was obsolete when the last nail was pounded. Our first four shelled corn bins were 1150-bushel Butler bins that were purchased new in 1953 from Goshen Implement. They were quite possibly the very first shelled corn bins in Indiana. Our on-farm storage grew to a peak of 110,000 bushels of grain storage.

Our crop acreage was increased and the yields grew due to irrigation. The last building added to the farm was a storage/grain dumping and drying setup. The construction followed a design that I turned in for my ag engineering 421 course at Purdue. I was fortunate to get the innovation gene from my father. Dad and I took great satisfaction bringing new ideas to fruition.

Shelling corn, storing shelled corn, the largest grain bins, the second farm in the region to irrigate in 1967 (we started two weeks after a farm in New Paris), machine harvested sweet corn, staked tomatoes, mulching vegetables, the first corn maze in the state, embryo transplanting, selling pregnant recipients, buying the first Angus pregnant recipient in the nation, selling corn shocks, pre-bagging sweet corn, "The Farmer's dozen", showing embryo cattle, county level blood typing of registered Angus in shows, the first farm in Indiana to use RFID tags, irrigated corn contest winners, record selling Indiana Angus futurity female, buying record selling Angus futurity bull (Car Don Westville), moving buildings, museum donations, one room schoolhouse moving and donating, tree planting, centennial celebration, fall displays, hay rides to the pumpkin patch, night hayrides and bonfires, Sweet Corn festivals, 'Corn Wars', farm tours, beef tours, founding and serving on many boards and organizations are all part of our farm's history and legacy.

One of the very first shelled corn bins, purchased 1953 Currently located at Crossroads Vet Clinic, Mottville, MI Picture circa 2022

Angus cattle...

A decision to join the Beef Club, which was part of the 4-H program, led us to owning registered Angus cattle. We bought my first Angus heifer at a consignment sale in Columbia City, Indiana in 1963. Our herd grew by retaining our 4-H heifers until they were raising calves of their own. In November of 1970 we bought a good heifer from Dave and Mary Hannon at the Black Harvest Sale in Valparaiso, IN. She went on to be the Champion Angus Heifer at the Elkhart County Fair the next summer. Beef cattle prices are very cyclical and our plan was to build our herd up during the low point of the cycle and have a production sale at the peak. A feed shortage in 1975, delayed our plan until 1979. We had a very successful sale and it propelled us into buying and selling purebred Angus, transplanting embryos and artificially inseminating our herd to prepare for the next cycle peak. We raised, sold, and exhibited champion steers and heifers. Our Angus herd was an important part of our farm operation. Owning cattle provides farmers with their savings account or rainy-day fund. By law, farmers have to be paid for livestock they sell within 24 hours. Emergency money was always one day away.

All of our children, Morgan, Samuel, Peter, and Alex were in Beef Club all ten years of their 4-H careers. The chores, making new friends, show day and sale day at the fair, the spider and euchre culture at the Beef Barn, and the Beef concession stand all provided life lessons for our children. Time management and the responsibility of caring for animals are just two of the valuable lessons learned. The Beef Club allowed members to show and sell two steers. The income earned from selling their steers easily eclipsed any amount earned from a 'normal' summer job. One year, we exhibited 8 Angus steers that we had raised. Glen Byler and Leon Tucker were agriculture icons in our area and they both complimented me on the quality of our cattle.

Their endorsement gave me more satisfaction than any ribbon or trophy. I enjoyed exhibiting our Angus cattle. We competed in local, state, and national shows. Our bulls sold in Michigan, Wisconsin, and Indiana Test Stations. The Centreville Fair, in Sturgis, Michigan, was always a treat at the end of the summer. It is held the third week of September. Our barn on the east side of CR 17 was where our handling facility was located and I spent many hours calving, clipping and washing cattle for shows. When my truck was at the barn, it served as an open invitation for friends and neighbors to stop in and see what was going on. One year, in early September, I was in the barn clipping on my best bull calf, getting him ready for the Centreville Fair. He was in the head gate and I was underneath him, clipping the long hair off of his belly. This is when I discovered two strips of white hair close to his front legs. This prevented him from showing as a registered Angus bull. Registered Angus cattle used to be able to have white hair on their entire underbelly. The Angus Association changed the rules at some point to restrict the location of white hair to only the rear of the navel.

Occasionally white hair would appear in front of the naval due to residual genetics popping up in an animal's haircoat. This was one of those situations. Denny Sharkey had stopped by the barn during this discovery and offered to buy him for his kids' 4-H steer, if the calf lived through the castration. The surgery on a calf that weighs 900 lbs. can sometimes be a difficult procedure. The calf could be shown as an Angus steer because he exhibited all Angus breed characteristics. It also helped that he had been bought from a local Angus breeder. The calf's sire was Byergos Black Revolution 36, who had a reputation of siring very desirable show cattle. The price of $900 was agreed upon and the steer survived the surgery. He won the Champion Angus Steer award the next summer. Denny passed away on October 22, 2025 during the writing of this book. He was a good friend.

Chapter Two

SOUTH OF THE FARM

The Frances Everest Farm...

Ben Everest owned quite a few acres in Jefferson and Concord townships. He owned the 80 acres directly south of the original Bullard 40 acres. Ben came to Dad in 1961 and suggested that Dad buy the 80 acres. Ben's sister, Frances, had been living in the farmhouse and she passed in 1959. There was a big barn on the property and a second, smaller house. Dad explained that he liked the idea, but he didn't have any money. Ben replied, "I will loan you the money." Ben must have had been a good judge of character and had tremendous confidence in my father. One day when I was in the barn, I noticed that the board sheathing for the barn roof was black on the inside. I was told that it was salvaged from a covered bridge that had burned. Inside the barn was a cedar silo. Silos were built inside barns to protect the feed from the elements and aid in feeding the animals that were housed inside the barn. Jerry Calloway's round barn south of Rochester, IN has a silo inside of his barn and Fred Kuntz's barn on CR 19 had one as well. These were the three that I knew existed. Dad offered Frances' farmhouse as housing for the families of our hired men as part of their salary. That was the case until Dad allowed my brother to live in the farmhouse.

Bill Wutrich, Dean Shue, Larry Minarik, Harry Myers, Jerry Yoder, and Jim Eastman were the hired men that I remember. The other smaller house was rented out and provided the first home for Beth and myself, Dean and Wanda Weirich, and Steve and Linda Garber. When the Eastside airport dissolved Dad bought one of the airplane hangars and moved the hanger, in three pieces, the two and a half miles and placed it west of Frances' barn. This hanger became known as the 'feedlot'. Pigs, Hereford cows, Holstein heifers, open beef heifers, Holstein bulls, Angus bulls and feeder cattle were all raised and fed at the feedlot. I dehorned my first cattle there, castrated my first pigs using turpentine and lard for wound healing, birthed, artificial inseminated cows and pretty much learned how to take care of animals at the 'feedlot'. Steve Hisey, a neighbor/friend/employee, and I dehorned 110 young Holstein heifers in one hour. We crowded the heifers into the feedlot's alley, like sardines in a can, and worked our way through the heifers. Steve held their heads and I manned the dehorner. We emerged from the task covered with blood that had spattered from their temporary wounds. Thinking the job would take much longer, Dad questioned why we had stopped? We told him, "We are done!"

Another feedlot story involved manure and the incident was funny at the time. At the west end of the feedlot, we had dug out the earth to allow for drainage of runoff and a collection pit for the manure until we were able to spread it onto the fields. The top of the slurry was crusted over and covered with small weeds. Randy Doering, another friend/summer employee, came running around the west end of the feedlot one summer day, and I could not wave my arms quick enough to prevent him from running waist deep into the smelly abyss. At the time it provided quite the laugh. I quickly found a hose and washed him down. Manure pits are now required to be fenced off, to prevent these types of accidents.

Another time, we had received a large amount of heavy spring snow and when I arrived at the feedlot to do chores, I found that a portion of the feedlot's roof had collapsed onto the pen where we were housing replacement beef heifers. As happens frequently on farms, the only heifer that was injured was the best one, a ¾ Simmental red with a white blaze. She had a broken leg and we managed to transport her to a processer to harvest the remaining meat. The roof repair was done fairly quickly. We used our loader tractor to lift the collapsed rafters and reinforced the structures with lumber that we had in storage. We also had a stack of corrugated roofing in one of our buildings that was needed to finish the repair. Many winter days, it was so cold that Dad and I would trade off feeding hay while the other would warm up in the truck. Frozen pipes were also a common winter occurrence. Hot water, torches, heat tape, heat lamps, and salamanders were all used to thaw out frozen pipes.

Maggot Hill...

When Dad purchased the Everest farm, he was cautioned by the county agent, that the land was classified as 'marginal' which meant it would be a constant struggle to produce a crop. What the agent was unable to foresee was the arrival of irrigation. One particular sand hill on the farm was literally only a waterfront away from being a beach. The soil's classification was Plainfield Sand. In the early seventies an unrelenting heat wave resulted in the daily loss of a substantial number of chickens from heat stroke. Fans, sprinkling irrigation water on the metal roofs, hourly walking the chicken houses to prevent the chickens from just laying down and dying were all unsuccessful in preventing hundreds of deaths. The sandhill rarely grew anything and even weeds struggled to grow. The hill was assigned as the final resting place for literally thousands of the dead chickens. Daily, we would load the back of one our pickup trucks with the dead chickens and shovel them off at the top of the hill. After several hot days the hill became alive and earned the name 'Maggot Hill'. Today, with the current commercial and residential development, it is hard to even imagine this disposal strategy. At that time, the only homes within a mile of Maggot Hill housed our employees or known neighbors. Years after the disastrous heat wave, Maggot Hill remains a landmark of the area.

In the mid-1970s, Indiana and Michigan Power Company informed us of their plan to build a high-power line across our farms. We opposed this construction because it would be very difficult to farm around the towers. They informed us that they already had an easement in place and there would be no compensation for any inconvenience or damage to the land or crops. The easement was obtained in the early 1900's and encompassed the entire farm. The power companies extorted farmers into signing these easements in return for bringing electricity to their farmstead. This was a common practice. The total compensation for the easement, into perpetuity, was $770. The power line was designed to cut across our farm on a diagonal path that included Maggot Hill.

At that time, we were using Vermeer stationary irrigators that had two 75' arms mounted on a trailer gear. We had four of these sprinklers that irrigated a 150' radius that were fed from the well by 20' long, 6" hook and latch aluminum pipe. Dad requested that the power lines across our farm be constructed at a higher elevation to avoid the possibility of our sprinklers coming in contact with the power lines. This request was denied.

Quite often, when the water was turned off to move the sprinklers to the next location, one arm would drain before the other and the result would be that one of the sprinkler's arms would tip up due to the weight imbalance and then settle to a level position once the water was drained. This was the fear. In the summer of 1974, the prediction came true. The sprinkler was at the peak of maggot hill, the water was shut off, the water drained, the arm went up and just caught the 144 kV power line. The southern half of the city went dark including the Concord Mall, south of Elkhart. Chain was welded together at the well head 1000 feet away. The above-ground aluminum irrigation pipe looked like it had been used for target practice. It was unbelievable that no one was killed. Workers on the farm were literally minutes away from contacting the pipe. The story continues...the day of the accident was the exact day that our farm insurance was being switched to another company. The old company's policy was in place until the end of the day. The new company's policy was set to take effect the next day. This is what was conveyed to Dad by the insurance agents verbally. Both verbal assurances were not true. The evidence exposed a 12-hour gap in coverage. The accident occurred during this gap in coverage. I was at Purdue at the time. The story was told to me that after legal involvement from all sides, the old insurance company ended up honoring the agent's verbal statements to my Dad. This incident taught me that all insurance companies carry "errors and omissions" insurance. The claim was covered by the company's policy.

The Farmer's Inn...

An important part of farm communities all over the world, is the presence of a gathering place for laborers and land stewards to eat breakfast. The most important meal of the day might take place in a home, a café, or an Inn. We ate breakfast at the Farmer's Inn. It was located on a dangerous curve, a little over a mile, south of our farm on U.S. Highway 20. At the Farmer's Inn, some customers started their day with breakfast, other farmers completed their chores before breakfast, and some just gathered to get neighborhood updates over a cup of coffee. The original name of the restaurant was the 'Brown Derby'. When Mrs. Martin bought the business in the seventies, she changed the name to the Farmer's Inn. Aggie and Doc owned it for a time either before or after Mrs. Martin. Aggie firing a gun at Doc, in retaliation for his philandering, was a rural legend.

Art and Betty Rogers were the last owners of the business before the State of Indiana took the land and business for the construction of the US 20 bypass. What few people knew is that the land and building were owned by Garber's Cottage Inn on Cassopolis Street. It was local knowledge that Mr. Garber's daughter was the actual owner. Art and Betty's settlement was so small it was embarrassing. The amount they received from the State was comparable to one Saturday of sales. The numerous stories about the Farmer's Inn included crashes, shootings, threats, and thefts. The biggest theft was the beforementioned theft by the State of Indiana when they took the land for a new road in 1991. The restaurant was located in the northbound lane of the current CR 17 under the US 20 overpass. Betty Rogers had a gift of being able to fill every seat, especially on a Saturday morning. She knew everybody and would introduce neighbors to each other and would ask them if they minded sitting with each other. I never witnessed someone refuse her persuasion. At the designated 'Farmer's Table' knowledge was dispersed, hyperbole challenged, and grief shared. In June 1991, the restaurant was demolished for the bypass construction and a neighborhood era ended.

The Adcock Family...

Leonard and Nancy Adcock had seven children, L.C., Charlie, Velma,

Bill, twins Raymond and Daymond, and Jack. They lived on a farm east of the Farmer's Inn on US 20. Their farm would have been located under the present day 'banana bridge' of the US 20 bypass. Everyone in the family was a hard worker and I think they all worked for Dad at one time or another. All of the boys definitely caught chickens. Like all families, their paths varied in length and width. Dad shared a story about Bill's paper route. Bill's bike chain had broken about ½ mile north of our farm and 9- year-old Bill walked his bike to our farm to ask Dad for a ride home. When Dad arrived at the Adcock home, Bill took his bike off the truck and asked, "What do I owe you, Herm?" Dad told that story many times and used it as a lesson for life. Bill was a self-taught quintessential renaissance man. He founded ADCO, a mechanical and electrical contracting company whose clients included everyone from homeowners to the government. He could sing, played many instruments and was a member of several bands. I remember Bill having a great sense of humor. After he survived a heart attack and the subsequent surgery, he bought a sailboat and took sailing lessons. He has sailed rivers, lakes, oceans, canals and has sailed around countries and islands.

Raymond and Daymond were twins and they were in my grade all through school. My memory is that they were a year older in age. They always seemed twice my diminutive size. They caught chickens and mowed our large farm yard with our push mower. They would trade off mowing and I remember them running while mowing. They baled hay and seemed to be 'on call' for any job when we needed extra labor. Raymond was naturally smart. For many reasons, there was not much home support for school. Discipline and a good dose of love were the main ingredients of their lives at home. At that time, most classroom seating was assigned by alphabetical order. I usually sat next to, or behind Raymond. As the graded quizzes and tests were passed down the row, I would consistently notice the 'A's' that Raymond would receive on his tests. His lack of completed homework would lower his grades to C's. He also provided a life lesson to me to not judge a book by its cover.

Raymond and Daymond would sometimes come to school dressed in the same clothes that they had caught chickens in the night before. My class was the last one to receive a draft number before the draft was abolished in 1972. Birthdates would be drawn by the lottery method and low numbers would get drafted into the army with the intent of being sent to Viet Nam for cannon fodder. My memory recalls Raymond's number was 11, mine was 182, out of the potential 365. Instead of getting drafted, Raymond volunteered for the Air Force. As far as I know, his education and knowledge of the airline industry was gained in the Air Force. After his service to the country, he started a wire harness business in Fort Wayne. He owned several planes and piloted the 767 before it was available for purchase by the airlines. At Leonard's funeral, almost all of his employees drove up from Fort Wayne to support Raymond and his family. His twin, Daymond, got mixed up with a bad crowd and his life was cut short. Instead of the novel "The Tale of Two Cities", their lives could easily be titled, "The Tale of Two Twins".

Jack, the youngest, always thought of my Dad as his second father and I always thought of Jack as a brother. Another story from my Dad, was one of the times he picked up Jack's older brothers to catch chickens, 5-year-old Jack came running out of the house, in his diapers, asking if he could go along. Jack was a constant presence around our farm. Catching chickens, driving tractor, helping with planting or baling hay, harvesting, irrigating, building something or helping with cattle. These were all tasks that Jack made easy. He worked at

Western Rubber until they closed and then he worked for a home construction company before starting Jack Adcock Construction. His skill constantly improved and he got the reputation of providing an excellent product. Jack can produce three hours of work out of an actual hour. I helped him build a few homes and he taught me to not waste steps, material, or time. He helped build our farm market, and built or repaired many of our farm buildings. He has retired from skiing and riding motorcycles but still enjoys fishing trips with his family. Joyce, was his neighbor until circumstances brought them together and they married. Jack asked Dad for advice on a potential purchase of a 40-acre farm. The decision to purchase that farm, and its later sale, made it possible for Jack and Joyce to retire and move to Tennessee. They live there today. Whether it was plowing snow, baling hay, building something or peeling icebergs off the side of a local factory, Jack was always our first call.

Arrowheads...

One of life's humbling and rewarding experiences, is the discovery of an Indian arrowhead lying on the earth. Your mind experiences a diverse and rapid thought exercise. Who made this? When was it made? Had it been discarded or used? If it was used, was its intended target an animal? Another Indian? A white man? How long did it take to form its shape? This illusive prize seems a fitting reward for anyone that has a strong bond with the land. I have learned that very few people have actually found these historic weapons. I have found countless pieces of the raw material, flint. These pieces of flint might have been discarded after being broken during construction. Some might have been broken by tilling implements. Many of my discoveries reside in numerous cardboard boxes. A few of my complete arrowheads have permanent places in my memory.

One such discovery was made on a day following a downpour of rain. It was a black, oblong shaped and about 3 inches in length. I was rolling up an irrigation hose with our M tractor and our hose reel on the main lane just north of the feedlot. There was a washout of sand, due to the rain, and upon looking down, the discovery was made next to the tractor's wheel. Another arrowhead discovery occurred during a check of our cow herd. I was walking along the farm's easternmost fence row next to the Pin Oak tree that was on the top of the hill. We had purposely left that tree standing for shade and it marked the ridge that the old Fort Wayne Road followed on the route from Elkhart to Fort Wayne in the 1800s. I noticed a small red stone next to the base of the tree and proceeded to scratch it out of the dirt. The stone was a near-perfect arrowhead about the size of a nickel. This size was commonly used for bird hunting.

Spraying applications on crops are routinely made at dusk or at night to minimize spray drift. During one such application, to prevent ear-worms on sweet corn, another 'find' was made. For a reason that escapes my memory, I stopped the tractor and got out of the cab and immediately found a white arrowhead shining against the dark dirt, illuminated by the tractor's lights. Another arrowhead discovery was in the field we called the '13 acres'. This particular field has a few more stories later in this attempt, but right now I will limit the topic to arrowheads. A method that we used in our years of vegetable production was the laying of plastic mulch. The plastic served several purposes, including weed suppression and moisture retention. Early in the plant's growth we could cultivate between the rows as well as straddling the rows with a tractor mounted cultivator. This eliminated small weed germination, covered small weeds, and greatly reduced herbicide use. One of these cultivations tossed another, near perfect, bird arrowhead up onto the black plastic where it was discovered after a few irrigation applications had washed away the soil from the edge of the plastic. The timing of arrowhead hunting is strategic and it is key to a successful outing. The ideal time is to embark on a hunt is after a downpour of rain. The ideal land is a field that has been freshly tilled and has a history of producing successful findings of arrowheads. My grandfather, Adam P. Beehler, taught me these strategies. After such a rain, the arrowheads seem to float to the surface. One day, Dad told me that he had decided to sell the '13 acres'. The removal of fence rows and the combining of fields, made the field actually, 27 acres, but we still referred to it as the '13 acres. I am certain that Dad worried what my reaction would be, as the land had been in the family for over eight decades. I replied that it was his land and his decision. I totally understood. Most farmer's 401Ks are the land and equipment that they had accumulated over their time farming. The sale enabled him to be debt free and financially secure at the age of 75. I remember him expressing his relief in the fact that he could walk to the mailbox without the fear of finding a bill that he couldn't pay.

Back to the arrowheads. As the developer's excavation began on the 13 acres, our underground irrigation pipe had not been removed as of yet. The value of the plastic pipe outweighed the expense of digging it up. With new gaskets the pipe could be reused. 'Johnny' was an employee of Niblock Excavating that was known to us and he was operating an excavator on the site for the developer. I walked across the barren field to ask him if he would leave the keys in the backhoe and allow me to use it to dig out the underground pipe after hours. While walking toward where he was working, I noticed the best arrowhead I have ever found lying on top of the yellow sand about thirty feet to the side of my path. It measured about 2" long and 1 ½" wide. It had been made by a very skilled artisan because it was crafted with twist to allow the arrow to spin during flight. Several arrowhead collectors doubted my claim of the rifling of the arrow until they examined the arrowhead. They all agreed that the twist in construction was intentional. It holds a spot on top of my bookcase where daily viewing is possible. When I talked to Johnny, he said he would dig the pipe out for us.

Arrowheads that I have found. Display frame made from salvaged sweet corn wagon floor. A gift from Erin Payne

The Pasture Field....

Located just south of US 20, on the east side of CR 17, there was another chunk of land we referred to as the 'Pasture Field'. This property was given to my grandfather, Roy, as part of the 'dowry' when he married my grandmother, Bernice Pollack. It was later passed down to my father. The land was divided into a tillable 17-acre field on the north end, a 7-acre tillable field on the southwest corner, and 29 acres of grass. A spring-fed pond was located in the middle of the grass pasture. Over the years, the pasture provided summer grass for turkeys, Holstein heifers, Angus cows and crossbred cows. One winter we even sheltered a herd bull on the pasture because we had no other place to isolate him away from the cow herd during the off season. We slid a small building on the snow-covered road the two miles from the farm to the pasture to provide him shelter.

Art Tate, commonly called 'Tater', lived on CR 17 across from the pasture field. One day, while I was checking cows, he walked across the road and told me a story about my grandfather. Tater said that when he was about 10 years-old he remembered leaning on the fence watching Roy till the 17-acre field. My grandfather stopped discing and asked Art if he wanted to drive the tractor. Art climbed onto the 8N ford tractor and Roy proceeded to teach him the dos and don'ts of tractor driving. Tater said he never forgot the kindness and willingness of my grandfather to teach him.

The 7-acre patch of the land shrunk in half when the county/state widened CR 17 and built the US 20 Bypass interchange. The area that remained was too hard to farm and the County had eliminated all practical entrances to that field with their widening design. After calculating the space, I decided to buy 650 tree seedlings from the Soil Conservation Service, during their spring tree sale, and plant them in that area. Tara Steede and I planted the trees in rows filling the entire area of land. A few years later we transplanted the nearly 2 feet tall tree starts along CR 14, CR 17, at the farm and at our house on the corner. Our children still remember hauling many buckets of water in a small wagon to those trees. Many of those trees are still standing today.

The cattle that grazed the pasture were provided water from the spring fed pond. It was originally dug with a horse-drawn slip scoop by my grandfather. This excavation allowed the spring to fill the man-made reservoir. In 1983, the pond completely dried up. Cattle without water creates an emergency. An extreme drought and years of erosion and manure accumulation were responsible for the disappearance of the water. After discovering the urgent situation, I called Niblock Excavating and they came to dig out the pond and reshape the banks. The very first bucket-full released pent-up pressure from the spring and water shot 3-4 feet into the air. We never had to dig the pond out again.

Our Angus cows in the spring on the Pasture Field

One winter, the pond provided us the opportunity to ride our snowmobiles across water. The trick was to get up enough speed to coast across the water to the other side. After countless trips across the water, we stopped, deciding the odds of continued success were getting smaller. The spring-fed pond is still there. Crossroads Church approached Dad in the 2000s about buying the land of the Pasture Field. They had conducted a demographic study and concluded that the location was ideal for the church's long-range growth plan. Their vision was to build a senior living community in conjunction with a new church building. The political power in Elkhart County is infected with developers and realtors. Most decisions are influenced by a handful of old, rich, white men. The senior living part of the development was denied. I surmised the denial was due to perceived competition with another similar development 20 miles away. The church was approved and the balance of the land was approved for office space which conveniently provided revenue source for builders, realtors, etc. etc. etc.

Land that we rented...

The Hartman farm laid up next to US 20 just south of our property line. I rented the farm from a developer after he bought the farm from the Hartmans. I extended above ground irrigation pipe to the farmland and grew sweet corn and pumpkins. It provided enough income to cover expenses and the rent which the owner/developer used to pay the property tax. A storage unit business is on that land today. A large percentage of land, that I farmed over the years, was in transition. Much of the land was owned by retired farmers or his heirs and was sold and developed into commercial or industrial properties. The developers would pay more than any farmer could afford to pay for the land and the developers could just wait for the big payday. The old saying, "it takes money to make money" is an excellent depiction of the entire east side of Elkhart. We used this technique a few times ourselves, mostly for the survival of the farm. We did quite a bit of custom spraying of farm fields in the 1970's. Our plan was to finish planting our crops early and then have a 3-4-week window to custom spray for other farmers. Greens, Gilreaths, Hoffmans, Lovejoys, Hochstetlers, Hostetlers, Reigseckers, Knepps, Gundermans, were all our spray customers. Many of these farmers rented their ground to me as they retired from farming. Dozens of landlords and many dozens of individual fields provided me with a recurring nightmare. I would wake in the middle of a winter night, haunted by the scenario that I had forgotten to harvest a field.

Chapter Three

WEST OF THE FARM

George Kile...

One mile west of our farm lived George Kile. He was widely considered the wisest man in the neighborhood. George was 65 years-old when I was born. He was the oldest man I knew until he died at the age of 101. One example of his quick wit and clear thinking involved my birth. I was born on January 2nd, 1954. My Dad was excited to tell George that he had a son born. He went down the mile to George's house and shared the news. Dad commented that if I had been born a few days earlier, he would have had a tax deduction for the previous year. George immediately quipped, "you'll have him an additional year chand you will need the deduction more then than you do now". George was a philosopher, a poet, advisor, and mentor.

Another story that was told is that he had been selected to play AAA baseball but stayed home to help the family farm. He attended the Union School, Concord District 12, going when he could, mostly in the winter, until he was 21. The schoolhouse was located across the road from our farm and now stands at Bonneyville Mill County Park in Bristol, Indiana.

George was the first farmer in the area to use the herbicide atrazine on corn. He came down to our farm to tell the results to my Dad and grandfather. He told them, "It looks like the weeds were set on fire!" George was a frequent contributor to the Elkhart Truth's editorial page and used pen names like A. B. See, Dan D. Lion, and I. Ben Thru. The following letter to the editor of the Elkhart Truth appeared in the paper, March 27, 1974.

> Disclosure, Before and After
> Hindsight
> We the people are getting tough
> We treat our politicians rough
> Before he can land a public berth
> He must disclose how much he's worth.
> A better law to spot the grafter
> How much before then and how much after.
>
> A.B. See

George made a promise to his dying brother-in-law that he would take care of his wife, George's sister, after his death. He received the farm in return for this promise. Many years later, most thought that George and Jenny were husband and wife when in fact they were brother and sister. In the 1960s, Banner Homes was a new trailer manufacturing company and they approached George with an offer to buy his farm and use it as a location to build their factories. He came to the farm to share the news and details of the proposal with my father. Dad asked him where he planned to move and live. George thought he would buy a piece of land and build a small house on it somewhere close. Dad knew from experience that when people make a move from a home they have lived in for years to a new place it can sometimes shorten their life. Dad suggested that George ask Banner if they would give him a life lease on his current farmstead and house. Banner took the offer. They probably assumed it would just be for a few years as George was in his late 70s. George outlived not only the Banner company but also the next two businesses that occupied those buildings. I rented 25 acres from George in the early 1980s; Oak Ridge Estates mobile home park is located on that land today. That first year turned out to be a bad farming year and the sandy soil proved unproductive.

That fall I went down to George's house with the intention of paying him the $750 that I owed him for the land rent. $30 per acre for unirrigated sandy ground was a fair price. I was puzzled when George asked how I intended to pay the rent, as I had not made any money off of the crop. The question was valid and he knew it was true due to his experience. "Why don't you wait until next year and see how next year turns out," he said. His character was overfilled with things that money can't buy. Another example of his quick wit and clear thinking involved his time as a bus driver for the Concord Schools. Many farmers were hired as bus drivers as a way to pay for their property taxes. George was Dad's bus driver from his first day of school. The bus had to travel a mile east of CR 15 to pick up just one student, my father. The school was aware that George knew our family and asked him to ask if my grandfather could bring young Herman down the mile to be picked up by the bus, thus saving the school 10 miles a week. George answered, "I have to pick him up, he is the only one paying his way!" He knew that the small homes along the route weren't paying enough taxes to pay for their children's schooling, where a farmer was paying enough taxes to pay for multiple students. George was a big influence in my life and helped me determine who I wanted to be living forward.

One of the buildings on George's farm was an icehouse. It was constructed with two feet thick walls that were filled with sawdust for insulation. There were many wood racks that held the sawn blocks of ice. George told me how he would take a wagon pulled by horses, in the early 1900s, one mile north to the St. Joseph River and saw blocks of ice from the frozen river, load them onto the wagon and haul them back to stock the icehouse. The supply of ice would last almost the entire summer. They provided safe food storage and extra income from the sale of ice blocks to neighbors. One of my few life regrets is that I didn't save and move the icehouse to a location beyond the reach of demolition.

During another one of my too few conversations with George, I mentioned that I needed to buy some straw for animal bedding. He said that there were some old bales up in his barn and if I wanted to dig out any bales, that the mice hadn't eaten the strings, I could have them for free. I climbed up into the hay mow on an unusual ladder that had angled steps. I inquired about the unusual design and learned that it was a log cabin loft ladder. George had wired it to the granary and he used it to climb up to the hay mow. George had a farm sale after he moved to live with his granddaughter. He had become extremely frail and was close to being home-bound. For some reason I missed the sale, and later that day I drove down to George's farm and found one of the auctioneers going through the unsold items. He told me anything that remained was free for the taking. I went immediately to the barn knowing the ladder was certainly gone. It was still there! I unwired it from the haymow and carried it to my truck and took it home. We used it to display our many quilts. A lifetime auctioneer had the opportunity to view the ladder in 2017. After a few moments, I asked him what he was thinking? He replied, "I think that is the oldest ladder I have ever seen." He aged it from the late 1700's. It currently is hanging in our courtyard in Phoenix.

A few of George's quotes that stick firmly in my mind mostly reference his aging. He wondered why "God was making an example of him." He also said "that if he had to pick 100 years to live in the history of man, it would be the 100 years that he lived." He said that he had, "stopped reading the obituaries because he no longer knew anybody that was listed." About farming, he said, "I know how to farm better than I have the money to do it." Arden Erikson, a reporter for the Elkhart Truth, wrote a great article about George that appeared in the paper September 17, 1989. Everyone that knew George Kile was thankful for his life lessons.

The East Side Airport

On the northwest corner of Middlebury Street and Middleton Run Road there was a small airport. The East Side Airport was operational for small planes until the mid-sixties. Dad farmed the blow-sand between the runways. Along Middleton Run Road there was a restaurant and a midget car sprint race track located across from present-day Mayberry Café. I barely remember these old landmarks. When the airport was sold for development Dad bought one of the airplane hangars and moved it down the road in three pieces and placed at the west end of the Frances Everest barn for our feedlot shelter. West of the airport there was a large tract of land owned by the Noble brothers. I think they were twins. Dad rented and farmed much of the land and I remember opening fertilizer and seed bags in the back of a flatbed truck and throwing dirt clods between planter fills. The Nobles offered to sell the land to Dad but the farming risk was too great he decided not to buy their property. The land was developed into commercial and industrial expansion over the next five decades and the Nobles retired multi-millionaires. More than once, financial pressures and traditions, imprison one's decisions.

Bullard Road today...

In 1960 Dad purchased land on the northeast corner of CR 14 and CR 15. At that time there was a ten-year program available through the USDA called the 'Soil Bank'. If a farmer enrolled land into the Soil Bank, he would receive annual payments to keep the land out of production. One of the requirements was that the farmer would establish grassland on those acres. The purpose of this program was conservation and to help keep crop prices at least higher than the cost of production. The goal was to help prevent farmers from bankruptcy. In our case, the payments that were received made the loan payments on the land purchase. The idle grassland provided a perfect environment for quail, pheasants, and rabbits. I was allowed at a young age to walk our dog, Belle, along CR 14 to the grassland and hunt for quail. We knew all the neighbors and all the people that traversed the roads around the farm. One of life's most exciting gifts is the thrill experienced when a covey of quail flushes, scatters and lands. It becomes a challenge to you and your dog to locate and acquire a single bird. In 1970 after the land completed its time in Soil Bank, Dad decided to build a road and sell lots to factories. He hired "Construction Dave" Bontrager to build the road base from CR 14 north and then west to CR15. Since Dad paid for and built the road, he decided to name it

Bullard Road, in honor of the original. Dave constructed the entire road without the use of a transit. The Dave Bontrager's that we knew included 'Big Dave', 'Produce Dave', 'Katie Dave', and 'Construction Dave'. As Elkhart moved east, several lots were sold. I farmed the small patches that were left between the factories until they were all sold. A feeling that is hard to describe is experienced when a farmer is the first or the last person to till a piece of land. I have had these feelings too often. Neil Young has a lyric in his song, Old Man, that goes "I been first and last, look at how the time goes past". Every time I hear that song it gives me pause, and I remember the farmland that I have known that will never be farmed again.

Lucky's....

The 40 acres directly west of the farm was owned by a man I only knew as Lucky. I believe it once was added to the original farm that my great grandfather and his mother Elizabeth bought in 1891, and at some time, they had to sell it off. Lucky camped in a small shack on the corner of the 40 acres on weekends while he worked the farm. He worked in town the rest of the week. I was told the story of Lucky walking down to the farm from his shack to talk with my grandfather. This happened during the heart of the depression, which would have made my father about 10 years-old. They were sitting on the porch as Lucky explained to them that he was behind on his taxes and would like to sell his 40 acres to my grandfather. He offered to sell the 40 acres for $800. Roy declined, admitting that he was also behind on his taxes and didn't need the burden of more land. I am unsure when that land became part of our farm. The field, that we continued to refer to as 'Lucky's, was where I was allowed to plant my first corn at the age of 14. Dad told me to get on the IH 450 and make a few rounds. I had ridden on the fender of the tractor for many acres before that and knew what gear to plant in, how to operate the throttle, use the brakes to turn and what hydraulic levers to use to raise and lower the IH 56 four row planter. Clarence Yoder stopped by the road where Dad was sitting in the truck and asked, "Who was planting the corn?" I was at the other end of the field and the only thing he knew was, that it wasn't Dad. When Dad told him it was me, Clarence couldn't believe that Dad would entrust such an important job to me. Dad told me told me later that he told Clarence, that I could plant straighter than he could.

The contents of Lucky's shack at the corner of the field were unknown to me. Many years later, I asked for permission from Dad to cut the lock on the door and investigate. I found an old platform-scales that was used years earlier on our farm, a wooden, feed hand cart, and the wooden doors that were originally used between the bedroom and the living room of the farmhouse. I restored and certified the scales and used it to weigh produce. Lucky's land currently is occupied by numerous factories and businesses.

The Orchard...

The field directly west of the farmstead was referred to as 'The Orchard'. I can only remember one apple tree and one pear tree. There are only a few pictures of these trees. The 1970s ushered in the fad of farming 'fencerow to fencerow' and these trees were removed. Fences were torn out and fencerows were removed to facilitate larger fields and larger equipment. In the 1800s, farms were very diversified. Fruit trees and orchards were commonplace on most farmsteads. Sustainability and survivability were one and the same. Those days are gone. In 2019, I discovered a wooden beehive that must have been used on our farm. It was above the old shop as we prepared for the farm's very first sale of equipment, vintage tools, and antiques that had been accumulated over the 130 years. I kept the beehive, restored it and I use the hive's frames for pictures instead of honey. The land directly west of #3 chicken house was part of the Orchard and received many years of chicken manure applications from the #3 chicken house. This remained the most productive land on our farm for decades after we stopped raising chickens.

Chapter Four

NORTH OF THE FARM

The Dull Estate...

In the late 1800s and early 1900s, Burns Stark owned the Bluegrass Farm just north of our farm and the farmstead was on the east side of CR 17. In the late 1800s, that stretch of road was just a one lane, dirt, tree-lined path. Burns sold the farm during the depression to Ralph Dull on land contract.

Bluegrass Farm on CR 17 north of Bullard Road Circa 1890

The rural legend was told that Burns was hoping Ralph would default on the contract and he would get the farm back. Burns never got the farm back. Ralph was resourceful and was aided by his daughter, Pauline and her husband Harley Pletcher. Ralph's farm rule was that they should be in the field by 7:00 a.m., after the chores and milking were completed. They milked their Jersey cows by hand and Pauline had the reputation of being the fastest milker in the area. She could produce inches of foam on top of the milk bucket with her speed of milking. Pauline milked 7 cows morning and then again in the evening. Most could only milk 3 or 4 cows during the same amount of time. Crop yields were terrible during the Dust Bowl years. Ralph had heard about some green forage west of Elkhart along the river where what now is Lexington Landing, Elkhart, IN. They would load two horse-drawn wagons with the tall grass and drive them back to the farm through the town of Elkhart. They would make two 20-mile round trips every day to the river bottom to hand-cut the tall rip gut grass. They would unload the grass bundles into the ensilage chopper that blew the chopped forage into their glazed-tile silo. This feed sustained the cows through the winter. When Dad was a teenager, he remembered looking across the road from our farm to the 20-acre field where Ralph pastured hogs. The price of hogs was so cheap that Ralph just let them multiply at will. Dad said that he was sure he could walk the entire length of the field 'never stepping on anything but a hog'.

Ralph could remember when the population of the United States was 50 million. Bill Adcock told me that Ralph taught him how to correctly make change on his newspaper route. He taught Bill to count the change backward from the amount charged to the amount given. Truly, a lost skill. When Dad would visit Ralph, I remember sitting on the worn cloth sofa in Ralph's living room. Before I was in first grade, Ralph rewarded me with pennies when I correctly multiplied and divided fractions. After Ralph passed, his grandsons tried farming the land for a time. After that, the land was rented out to several different famers.

In 1979, the Dull estate was put up for sale. At that time, there was a new, unfunded program available through the Farmers Home Administration that allowed approved, young farmers the opportunity to buy farmland at 5% interest. The bank interest rates were 18-21%. My brother and I got approval for this program and bought two parcels, Dad purchased one parcel, and a local real estate broker, Erv

Gildner, found a buyer for the remaining parcels. I rented those parcels and farmed them for 42 years. We took out an unsecured loan from Shipshewana State Bank to put money down on our purchase while we waited for the loan program to be funded by Congress. The funding process was slow and the bank examiners were getting nervous about the unsecured loan. I decided to write our Senators and Congressman requesting their help with the federal government. Soon after I had sent the letters, the director of our local FmHA office wrote us a letter stating that the funds were available. Privately he admitted that he was told to take our application and place it on the top of the pile. Again, the saying, "It's not what you know, but who you know" proved true. One of the parcels that we purchased was the 20 acres directly across from our farm. We used that acreage to grow corn, sweet corn, pumpkins, Indian corn, green beans, wheat, and rye. In 1988, my brother, Dad, and I formed a partnership and built Bullard Farms Market directly across from our farmstead. That partnership worked great until it didn't. The rest of the land on that parcel was divided and developed into commercial businesses.

The Blue Grass Grange...

The original use of this building was a one room schoolhouse. It was built on the northeast corner of Bullard Road and County Road 17. It was named 'Union School, Concord School District 12'. It is my understanding the name 'Union School' was chosen because students from Washington, Jefferson and Concord townships attended the school. My grandfather, grandmother, and great uncle all attended this school along with many of our neighbors. Our farmstead was located directly across the road from the school and my great-grandfather, Phillip, would walk across Bullard Road to supervise recess. In 1913 the schoolhouse was no longer needed and the building and small parcel of land was purchased by the Grange Organization and was named The Bluegrass Grange No. 2191. Burns Stark's farm was directly to the north and their farm was named the Bluegrass Farm. A Jersey cow is centered on a hand-painted poster that commemorated the Blue Grass Grange's 25th Anniversary in 1938. During moving the building, I found the 3' x 4' poster in the attic of the building. We have it framed and displayed in our library next to where I am sitting, writing this book. The Grange is a national organization that was formed in 1867 to provide agricultural communities a place to share new ideas and provide support to families that were trying to survive. When the Bluegrass Grange disbanded, the small parcel of land and the building were sold at auction in 1972. Dad bought the Grange Hall building, I believe, for $10,000. We used it to store antiques, seed corn, necessary and un-necessary farm collectibles and tools. When I became a Jacques Seeds supervisor, we used the Grange to store the seed corn that was to be delivered to my customers. A common promotion practice of seed corn companies was to give small packets of sweet corn seed to their customers. At the end of the 1982 sales season, I had quite a few packets left and decided to plant 12 rows of "Jacques 87" just east of our #2 chicken house. It turned out to be a great year for sweet corn and we were able to give fresh sweet corn to our family, friends, and literally everyone we knew. Dan Logan, a family friend and neighbor, suggested that the sweet corn was so good he thought we could sell it. We took Dan's advice and our first attempt to sell our sweet corn was at a location about 4 miles east of the farm at a busy intersection. When that location failed to produce many sales, Dad said, "if we aren't going to sell any corn, we might as well not sell any closer to the farm!" We moved the hay wagon to the corner and set up to sell in the shade of the oak trees next to the Bluegrass Grange. We learned many lessons at that hay wagon. You will learn about my Mom inventing pre-bagged corn, when you read about 'The First Marilyn', later in this attempt. Dad also invented the 'Farmer's Dozen'. He wanted to beat the 'Baker's Dozen' and placed 14 ears in our bags. This solved several issues. If someone came up to the pile of sweet corn and proceeded to select their own ears, we could assume that they were a new customer. Given the choice of selecting only 12 ears or having us bag 14 guaranteed ears, very few customers bagged their own corn. This protocol basically eliminated all complaints. Even if by chance, there was one small ear or one small worm, customers rarely complained because they felt they got a deal receiving 14 ears in their dozen. When a customer would tease us about our miscounting, Dad would retort, "We aren't very good at math!" The south side of the Grange Hall also served as our marquee. The white painted background on old 4x8 sheets of plywood made a good contrast to the John-Deere-green words that were painted on the signs with a 3" wide paint brush. One sign touted whether we had yellow, bicolor or white corn that day. Other signs informed the days of the week and hours that we were open.

The Grange Hall used as our marquee

We used code numbers for our main varieties of sweet corn... 87,75, 309. All of these utilitarian gimmicks seem to add to the mystique of our brand...Bullard Farms Sweet Corn. After we built Bullard Farms Market, the Grange Hall building was used for farm storage, but it remained our billboard.

The Grange Hall's next act was to play the part of a bargaining chip in our battle with Elkhart County over the widening of CR 17. In 1991, we lost a house, 12 acres, 13 road entrances, and 7 summers of normal business at our market to eminent domain. We came close to losing the Grange Hall building that served as the first schoolhouse of my grandparents and many of the neighbors. When the widening of CR 17 was first proposed, it provided an opportunity for the Republican infected county officials to place their boot heels on our family's collective (minus one) necks.

Their original verbal promise was that they would condemn and 'take' the Grange Hall in accordance with the 5th Amendment to the Constitution, which allows taking of private property for public use through eminent domain. The County verbally promised to sell it back to us for $1. We could move it, sell it, or dismantle it.

As previously noted, the entire project called for obtaining a total of 12 acres of our land. Mom and Dad, Beth and myself, my brother and I, and Bullard Farms Market were all separate entities that were being dealt with to acquire the necessary land. We offered to combine these entities into one decision making group. I believe in 'tearing off the rear-view mirror', but this decision proved to be a bad decision. We should have resisted at every turn. After lawsuits, countersuits, studying eminent domain, mediation, stress and many sleepless nights; we were close to an agreement. The county, at the eleventh hour, threatened to demolish the Grange Hall unless we agreed to their terms. We reminded them that the deal was to sell it back to us. They acknowledged the offer, but countered that "it wasn't in writing". Dad held me back as I rose to kick the County attorney's ass. I had already arranged for Laraway Movers to move the building about 1000 feet to the northwest onto our property and immediately started racking my brain on ways to save the building.

The County had contracted Warner Construction to demolish the building and they had it scheduled for the day after Labor Day 1994. The week before scheduled demolition, my son, Sam, was with me in the market and overheard us discussing the dilemma. He asked, "Why don't you just talk to the guys tearing it down?". My ten-year-old son just turned on the light bulb! We had known the owners of Warner Construction for a long time and the normal protocol for right-of-way demolition was to quick claim deed the property to the construction company, thereby limiting the governing body from liability. A phone call to Warner confirmed that this was the case and after relaying the story to them they agreed to sell the building to us for $1.

They said if it wasn't there, they would not have to tear it down. I drove over to their main office and got a bill of sale. I warned them of possible repercussions from the County and they just laughed. At that time, they were the only game in town. I hired Bob Kindel, of Kindel Excavating, to remove the wings of the building with his mini-excavator. That left just the original school footprint for the move. I contacted Laraway to confirm the move date of Saturday, Labor Day weekend.

Thursday night, about 10:00 our phone rang. Beth answered and told me it was Laraway...my heart sank. I was certain a glitch occurred in the plan and the building would be lost. As it turned out, their employees had requested Saturday off. This would enable them to enjoy a longer holiday weekend. They wondered if it would be alright to move their equipment down yet that night and start at 6:00 the next morning. Whew!! Donuts, coffee, dozers, backhoes, pictures, video, hydraulic jacks, dollys, I-beams, and wood blocking were all part of the move and by 6:00 p.m. they were loaded and leaving with the Grange Hall saved.

The move exposed the foundation that was built four-foot-wide and made of stacked fieldstone. The building was just sitting on the foundation and it was not fastened down in any way. The row of oak trees, on the west side of the building, must have been purposely planted as a wind break. The hydraulic control panel kept the building level during the move and it also weighed the building at 47,000 pounds. Only one brick fell from the top of the chimney during the move and an empty coke can that was sitting on the threshold never moved as the building was towed across the field to its new location.

Toward the end of the day, while we were standing in the empty lot where the building had stood for 100 years, a car pulled up, a man got out and started to cry. He told me that his family had held their family reunions in the Grange Hall for many, many years and he couldn't believe the County would tear down such a historic building. He obviously had been following the saga in the newspapers and he was overjoyed when I told him that we saved it and showed him where we had moved it. We had beaten the County.

Politicians hold grudges, and thirty years after the move they are still POed. I had a few weeks to pour the footers and lay up the block foundation before we lowered the building. This would allow the removal of the beams and blocking. My ideas for the future of the building included a restaurant, a museum, a gift shop or other retail possibilities. Those ideas were soon to be superseded. As I was driving by the schoolhouse one day, I noticed several cars parked out in the field by the schoolhouse. I pulled up, walked in and found Ron Schmanske,

Brent Curry, and Randy Myers inside the building. Ron worked for the Elkhart Truth; Brent was a friend of Dad's and served on the Elkhart City Council.

I knew Randy from my first day of school as we rode the same school bus. Randy was a local architect. They told me they were on a committee charged with finding and moving, or constructing, a one room schoolhouse. The schoolhouse was to be located at Bonnyville Mill County Park. This building would provide a venue for fourth graders to study Indiana history and give them the experience of an early classroom setting. Elkhart County students were being bussed to Marshall County for this field trip. The plan was to provide a place in Elkhart County. Ron said they were there to examine the building's construction. They had been told that my schoolhouse was not available for purchase. I am under the assumption that a family member had told them that this was the case. We all know people that feel the need to speak for others, even when they have no knowledge of the circumstances. I responded that I was surprised of that information because no one had talked to me and I owned the building. Dad had given the building to me before the move with the confidence in my ability to save the school.

After learning about my ownership of the schoolhouse Ron asked, "if the building was for sale?". I replied, "No". I told him we would donate it. I followed Ron back to his office at the Truth and drew up a very short and simple bill of sale for $1. In the following months, the committee found out that 80 electric lines would have to be raised or temporarily taken down to facilitate moving the entire building to Bonnyville. They decided instead to dismantle the school and reconstruct it, at the park.

The Union School stands at Bonneyville Mill Park today and provides a location to study Indiana history and it can be rented out for events. In the 1960s, Concord Schools was in the process of demolishing their 6th grade building, which stood on the corner of Mishawaka Road and US 33. Mom and Dad happened to drive by as they were tossing school desks out of the upper floor windows into a refuse bin. These were the old Eclipse desks with the fold up seats and the ink wells in the top of the desks. Mom had Dad stop and she asked if she could save some of the desks. The construction workers said yes. When they got back to the farm, Dad walked to the pickup truck and Mom told him no, they needed to take the big truck. They loaded up approximately 75-100 desks and brought them back to the farm and stored them in the end of the basketball court in the big barn.

After many years of gifts given, and distribution to friends and family there remained 39 desks at the time the school was relocated. I prematurely offered the desks for use in the school. I had to withdraw the offer when Mom told me that she had planned on giving 13 desks each, to Michelle, my brother, and myself. My brother sorted his desks out and roped them off with caution tape, Michelle donated seven of her desks, and I donated my share to be used in the classroom at the Bonneyville One Room Schoolhouse. On a side note, my sister, Michelle, was a member of the County Park board at the time. The Schoolhouse Committee and the park board had to get approval from the County Commissioners to place the building at the park. The park department was leasing the park's land from the County. At the meeting, according to Michelle, a county commissioner was adamant that 'not one county dime' would be available to use on this project. The committee had already raised the funds needed and the approval was granted.

The Schoolhouse at Bonneyville Mill Unknown artist

The tractor accident...

In 2016, Tom Dull shared this story. Tom is a grandson of Ralph Dull. Tom was a neighbor and friend. Tom and his brother, Fred, were at the Bluegrass Farm and Fred was trying to crank start their grandfather's International H tractor. Fred gave up and walked across the field to their house on CR14. 13-year-old Tom stayed behind and took it upon himself to keep trying to start the tractor. He got it started, hopped on, got it into 5th gear, and throttled it up. His youthful exuberance yielded an accident caused by turning too fast with the loader bucket raised halfway. This resulted in the tractor flipping on its side and Tom being pinned under the tractor. His grandma, Tillie, was at the kitchen window and witnessed the whole ordeal. Ralph came running out of the house, angry and told Tom, "I ought to leave you there!" Tillie went to the phone to call for help. Those were the days when everyone was on a 'party line'. When she picked up the receiver, she found that my Mom was on the line. After telling the quick story, my mom hung up the phone and Tom's grandma proceeded to call someone for help. My Mom informed Dad, and Tom recalled that it seemed like just a short time had passed when Dad arrived at the upended tractor. Tom remembered seeing my Dad's red 5-buckle boots from under the tractor. Dad leaned over and asked, "Tom, are you dead?" A few people gathered including Tom's dad, and Fred, who had come back to the farm. Ralph had gathered some boards to help pry and Dad told Fred to grab Tom's feet and pull him out when he gave the go ahead. Dad positioned everyone in their spot and gave the command "one, two, three, heave!" The tractor raised up and Tom's brother pulled him out from under the tractor. Tom's only injury was a broken arm.

The tornadoes...

In the spring of 1938, a tornado destroyed the original Bluegrass Farm barn. In June of 1988, I was loading and sorting cows to take them to a registered angus sale in Illinois. I was in our cattle barn that was about ¾ of a mile south of the Bluegrass farm. A storm came up very quickly, and I went outside the barn to witness another tornado touchdown at the exact location it had 50 years earlier. There was limited destruction but it required attention during harvest to be on the lookout for wood pieces and tin roof sections that had blown into the field. Palm Sunday, April 11, 1965 produced many tornadoes across the Midwest. The infamous double tornado was also a product of this storm outbreak. Fred Flury, an Elkhart Truth photographer, captured the picture of this phenomenon. Dad ushered us all into the basement as he watched a tornado develop from our front porch. He called me upstairs to see the funnel cloud. It was so mammoth, it seemed like it was at the southwest end of our farm. The black, stack shaped, cloud touched the ground and it was suspended from a dark cloud bank positioned one third above the horizon. We could see debris in the air and Dad was certain our farm was directly in its path. He called the rest of the family up from the basement and hurried us into our grey Oldsmobile. We took off at a high-speed, traveling directly west, perpendicular to the path of the monster storm. We were out of the path of the storm in seconds and returned to the farm soon after, when he thought it was safe. We were prepared to see the farm totally destroyed. The only damage was an empty chicken feed bulk bin that had blown over. The next day we retraced the path of destruction and discovered that the funnel cloud we had witnessed was actually six miles away. The Sunnyside neighborhood had been completely destroyed. The deadly storms caused dozens of deaths and millions of dollars of property damage.

I was aware of two very different reactions to the damage that the Palm Sunday tornadoes caused. Ben Everest always tried to avoid three expenses; taxes, insurance, and interest. Ben lived on CR 117 just a few miles southeast of our farm. When he made it back from the safety of his daughter's basement to view his farm's damage, he found nothing. His entire farmstead was gone. No clean-up was needed; it was all gone. The house, the barn, the trees...everything was gone. Ben commented that he was tired of paying taxes on that old barn anyway. Alex Schweisberger, a relative who lived in neighboring St. Joseph County, left his basement after the storm cleared and saw that his barn had been destroyed by the tornado. He fell over dead from a heart attack.

The Valley Line Stop and the Chevy vs Ford drag races...

Normally, we ate breakfast at the Farmers Inn, but on Sunday mornings a group gathered at the Valley Line Stop restaurant at the corner of

CR 17 and SR 120, 1 ½ miles north of the farm. The name originated from the old stone building being a stop on the interurban rail line between Elkhart and Bristol, Indiana. Dan Logan and Ted Sautter were regular members of the breakfast gang on Sunday mornings. Ted was a Ford guy and Dan was a diehard Chevy guy. Quite often they would schedule a Sunday morning race to establish which brand of truck was superior. They would enlist Jim Swinehart, a local mechanic and Sunday breakfast regular, to stop south bound traffic at the Railroad tracks about one mile north of CR 14. At that time, there were no curb cuts, no factories, no houses, and little, to no, traffic at 6:00 a.m. Sunday morning. The unimpeded challenge would start at our corner and they would race to the tracks. After the race they would head to breakfast at the Valley Line, where the results would be debated and bragged about to whomever would listen. This challenge and the failure to win led to more than a few new truck purchases. A new truck would lead to another race. I am not sure when they stopped racing but more development, more traffic, and safety concerns all played a role in the decision to end the game. The Valley Line Stop eventually leased their land to McDonalds.

Chapter Five

EAST OF THE FARM

The three little pigs...

During our pumpkin raising years, our hayrides to the pumpkin patch and straw tunnel moved from the Market location to our farm on the east side of 17. Safety and liability were the main reasons for the move, along with one other reason. The farm location allowed for more bus parking, a farm animal petting zoo, and a corn maze. I believe our corn maze was a first in the State of Indiana.

We bought two pot-belly pigs to add to our group of goats and Jake the pony for our petting zoo. I can't remember if we bought the pot-belly pigs at the Walkerton livestock auction or privately. They provided enjoyment to the children and families that visited our pumpkin patch.

Just a few days after the pigs had settled into their new pen, the female gave birth to three little piglets. The male hog was immediately sold, because hogs can be very territorial and sometimes cannibalistic.

The three pot-belly piglets were a big attraction for the hayride customers and their antics produced much laughter. The three quickly became uncontrollable teens. Late one afternoon, I got a call from a neighbor who lived in the Bristol Hills, which were located two miles east of the farm. The woman on the phone asked if we happened to own three piglets.

The trio was in the process of tearing up her yard and flower beds. I told her to go outside and yell at them to go home, and minutes later I saw the three travelling back home at full speed, right down the middle of CR 14. I paid for the damage that they had caused by decorating her yard with one of our fall displays, corn shocks, pumpkins, mums, and Indian corn and gave her coupons for free sweet corn to use the next summer.

The muck...

One of the Dull estate land parcels that we purchased was 80 acres of muck which was located ½ mile east of our farm on the south side of CR14. An unwritten rule that I had learned from the old farmers in the area was, 'that if it was dry enough to work the soil in the muck...you better be working in the muck'.

Plowing, discing, dragging, planting, cultivating, or spraying; whatever needed to be done, the muck was always on the front burner if it was dry enough to work the soil. The elevation was so low that it was a constant challenge. In the mid-eighties several rows of my corn in the dead furrows and several acres in the back of the field froze off on July

7th. Truman Miller was farming the Polanski farm and had 40 acres of corn frozen that morning.

That particular field is the lowest point in Elkhart County. I was one of the handful of farmers that farmed the entire 80 acres of muck in one season. The field was bordered by ditches on all sides. In 1991, spring planting was delayed on the muck long enough to prevent the planting of regular field corn and we decided to plant sweet corn due to the shorter season needed for sweet corn. It turned out to be a good decision, until it wasn't.

Germination, rainfall, insect control, and maturity were all in the favor of a potential good crop. The start of the harvest was going to coincide with Labor Day weekend. This was always a good time to have sweet corn ready to sell. We were all set for harvest and Harley suggested that we move the sweet corn picker and wagon down to the field the day before. This would allow an early start the next morning. That night it rained 4 inches. Harvest was not going to happen and it seemed the entire crop would be lost. It was impossible to drive any piece of equipment across the saturated soil.

A brainstorming discussion yielded an idea from Dad. He said, "We could harvest it with horses." Larry Miller, one of our workers, suggested that we could use his family's horses to pull the wagons. The idea immediately took hold. Larry was one of our top workers for many years and most of his Amish family worked for us at one time or another. He thought his dad, Elmer, would let us use their two Belgian draft horses. It was off-season for the horses to work their farm. The work would be good for the horses, along with the advantage of having someone else supply their feed for a few weeks.

After we obtained Elmer's approval, we brought the horses, harnesses, and a hitch cart to our cattle barn on the east side of CR 17. We proceeded to assemble a crew of hand pickers to harvest the ready-to-eat ears. The local newspaper got wind of our endeavor and wrote a story including a photo about the dilemma and our solution. Amish were not allowed to have their picture taken and some of the workers hid in the corn rows during the picture taking. One morning while we were picking the sweet corn with horses, it was ironic when we saw a huge, tracked-up seed corn harvester traveling down CR 14 headed to a seed corn field that had suffered the same deluge. The two ends of corn harvesting technology were working in the same area.

I don't think it is a coincidence that the word 'muck' rhymes with the word 'stuck'. Almost every season there was a possibility of getting stuck in the muck. The process of extracting a tractor or implement from this type of predicament is a very dangerous operation and has been the cause of many farm injuries and deaths. Most wet fields have different soil characteristics depending on the amount of moisture present in the soil profile. One tactic to prevent getting stuck is for the farmer to realize the situation and make evasive maneuvers, before it is too late.

Back in the day, before radios or phones, I would end up walking back to farm for help after gaining this knowledge. Failure to raise an implement quick enough would also result in becoming stuck. Two options can be used once this mistake has occurred; the tractor driver can raise the implement, throttle up the tractor and spin through the wet area, or stop, raise the implement, lock it in the raised position, unhook the implement, drive the tractor to a dry area and use a cable or chain to pull the implement to dry ground. The implement can be reattached and start the farming operation again.

Discs, tractors, drags, planters, seeders, combines, and sprayers have all been victims of getting stuck in our muck field. I was planting corn in the Pine Creek East field which was across the road from the muck when our neighbor's hired man walked over to me to ask if I could help pull him out as he was stuck. I asked if he wanted me to call his boss. He replied, "I can't do that, he is planting corn!" I unhooked my planter, pulled him out and gave him a lesson in fitting the muck.

No injuries ever occurred during our 'stuck' adventures, other than the injury to the operator's pride. Larger, wider, faster farm equipment have made tillage of wet fields easier but if the big equipment gets stuck the options for extraction are limited. Burning brush or fence rows were also hazards that can result in catastrophe.

Due to the soil's high organic matter, the soil itself can catch fire and burn deep into the ground for decades. Dad always warned "never build or burn on the muck!" The deep peat and lack of solid, soil sub-strate made buildings vulnerable to long term construction instability. Wise words are ignored by the foolish. One spring, the muck's ditch along CR14 filled to the brim.

I discovered the cause was debris clogging the tile at the west end of the ditch. I cleaned out the debris and the ditch and the lateral ditches started to drain. Following the route of the field tile, I discovered that the tile drained into Pine Creek.

The end of the tile was also clogged and needed cleaning to allow the tile to flow. The discovery that both ends of the tile were open proved that it was not a field tile. Dad said he used that tile water as a source for drinking water for 60 years not knowing that it was an open drain and subject to road runoff, fertilizer over-spray, animal feces, and trash decay. It must have supplied him with some natural immunity as he lived until the age of 88!

Harley and Pauline Pletcher...

Harley and Pauline Pletcher were family friends and neighbors. Pauline was Ralph Dull's daughter and she and Harley worked on the Bluegrass Farm. My Dad described Pauline as the fastest hand-milker in the area. She was tasked with milking 7 cows morning and evening when others only could milk 3 or 4 in the same amount of time. She could always get the most milk out of the cow and her speed of milking usually produced an inch or more of foam on top of the milk bucket.

This story has been told previously in this book and it is worthy of the twice-telling. Harley and Pauline were involved in a story with Mom and Dad while sledding down the Mishawaka Hills in the late 1940s. They loaded up their toboggans and sleds and drove to a popular hill on Dragoon Trail. Dad headed down the hill on a toboggan. Their plan was to jump on his back, forming a human stack, as he passed by. Harley, then Pauline, and then Mari piled on top of each other. Their combined weight resulted in Dad breaking several ribs. The evening of sledding was cut short.

I never knew Harley very well until he started picking sweet corn for us. After hand picking 147 acres of sweet corn in the hot, dry year of 1988, we searched out the possibility of using a mechanical harvester. There were farmers that were removing the husking beds of old ear corn pickers to pick sweet corn mechanically and there were farmers fabricating elevating belts on wagons to allow the hand pickers to ride on a platform instead of walking. Byron Manufacturing was experimenting with a mounted prototype and in the winter of '89,

Dad flew down to Homestead, Florida to check out this new way of harvesting sweet corn. During the harvesting Dad suggested a few additions to the prototype that the company used a few to improve the machine. The ear saver bars and the addition of a blower were his ideas that were incorporated into the design.

We purchased one of the very first machines and mounted it onto our IH 856 tractor. Harley had helped harvest some of our handpicked corn by driving one of our ford tractors, and Dad thought he would be a good fit to drive the picker as he had a great deal of experience picking ear corn. For the next ten summers Harley and I worked together literally every morning during sweet corn harvest. If the morning's harvest went smoothly, we would take a break, about 6:00, and eat breakfast together at the Mayberry Café. If the morning's harvest presented an equipment breakdown or the sweet corn variety was difficult to harvest, we would take turns going for breakfast. Many mornings we would have 5 or 6 wagons loaded with Bullard Farms Sweet Corn by 7:00 a.m.

Harley Pletcher picking Sweet Corn

One day, in the market, a customer asked me when his particular bag of corn had been picked. I replied, "3:30." He then asked, "why do you wait until the afternoon to pick the corn?" I replied, "No, the other 3:30." I never saw Harley move quickly doing any task but somehow, he was always a step ahead of everyone else.

Many, many mornings he had the tractor's oil checked, the windows squeegeed of morning dew or scraped from a fall frost, the 856 was started, a wagon hooked up and ready to go. In the afternoons he would come back to the farm, top off the fuel tank, wash the picker, grease the bearings, and oil the roller chains. If the field we were picking was adjacent to the farm, he would be in the field starting on the first load by 3:30. Part of our farm worker training was learning where to locate the empty wagons in the field.

The empty wagons needed to be parked in a location that would give the tractor driver the easiest route to back up and hook up the wagons. We had rigged a rope to pull up the hitch pin on the full wagons.

Another necessary skill was to master the ability to time your arrival in the field for the exchange of wagons so that Harley didn't have to get out of the tractor. It usually took a few tries at correct wagon placement but Gene Herschberger, Erin Payne, Larry Miller, and Tara Steede were all masters at this task. They were a large part of our farm's success. They were tasked with many farm chores and jobs at the beginning of each day. Those four could run any business in the country.

The only days that Harley would only ask off was over Labor Day weekend. He participated in an annual trail ride/wagon train in Southern Indiana. Harley would load Jack and Jill, his miniature mules, their tack, and their wagon into his truck and his horse trailer and head to the trailhead. The trail ride schedule included arrival at camp, campsite set up and daily trail rides. Each day the riders and wagons would leave the camp and return by evening.

Harley would sleep in the uncovered wagon at night. The riders would share stories and food around the campfire each evening. I never went along, I should have. I believe Pauline only went one time. During a river crossing, the year she went along, their wagon tipped over in the current and the contents and all of the passengers emptied into the river.

Everyone was recovered safely but I imagine this this episode weighed on Pauline's decision to make that trip her first and last. Harley was picking corn one day and Tara Steede was helping him with the wagons.

She drove back to the farm without a corn wagon and asked me how many 'nitros' Harley was supposed to take. Harley carried nitro pills in a small metal tube and took one when he was experiencing heart pain. I told her that he was supposed to take one pill. She said that she saw him take four.

Later that morning, after he had gone home, I went to his house and we agreed that he should probably retire from picking corn. We both cried. A few years after Harley and Pauline had both passed, Beth and I got a new puppy, an Aussie-doodle female. Our name search was difficult as we searched through the lists of popular dog names. Beth asked "What about Harley?". The name fit perfect. I get to spend every day with her, remembering my friend, Harley Pletcher.

Alex, Herman, Sam, Kurt, Harley, Peter and Morgan Harley's wagon and Jack and Jill

Mike Foreman...

Mike Foreman was the general sales manager for Bill Elsey Olds and Cadillac. The dealership was located on the west side of Goshen Avenue just north of Middlebury St. in Elkhart, IN. That location is a little outside this book's intended parameter, but Mike's stories filtered east. In the 50s and 60s the middle class in Elkhart drove Oldsmobiles and the upper crust drove Cadillacs. Mike could sell an ice cube to an Eskimo. He lived by the mantra 'work hard, play hard'. He always had someone in mind that needed your car. During a trip to Bill Elsey's service department, Harley and Pauline stopped by the sales floor to say hi to Mike. Their car was being serviced before they took a trip to Florida. Mike was the type of person that people gravitated towards and those that knew him always stopped by the sales department to say hello.

As Harley and Pauline walked by the sales floor on their way to the service department, Pauline noticed a teal-colored, Olds Delta 88 with a white interior. Pauline was taken by the car and Mike sensed her affection. "That's the car you need to take to Florida!", Mike exclaimed. Harley and Pauline were farmers and a new car was not in the realm of possibilities. Mike told them that he knew of someone that needed their car and he could give them a great deal. They successfully avoided the offer by telling Mike they had some errands to run. When they returned home from their errands, they raised the garage door and saw the Olds 88 parked in their garage. It was washed, waxed, and full of gas. They drove to the dealership and traded in their car. Harley never learned how Mike got the car into their garage.

We plowed snow in the winter for extra income and had several snow plow trucks. One of our snow removal customers was Bill Elsey's dealership lot. Dad shared this story. If you have plowed snow, you know that it is a mistake to get too close to a wall or garage door with an angled blade.

Any ice, heavy snow, or imperfection in the asphalt will launch your truck and blade right into the wall or garage door, damaging property. Dad was plowing the first pass along the many garage doors of the service department and Mike was shoveling the remaining snow away from the doors. The next pass would result in pavement free of snow. It was cold and Mike had his slip-on rubbers over his wingtip shoes along with his hat, gloves and an overcoat covering his white shirt and tie. Several salesmen were watching from the large windows of the salesroom floor.

Mike flagged Dad down on one of his back-and-forth trips and motioned for him to roll down his window. "Look at those lazy sons-of-bitches," Mike said. "I've got four orders for Cadillacs here in my pocket and if one of those stupid bastards would come out here and help shovel, I would give them the orders. Herm, you know who is going to keep those orders?...ME!"

Mike never shied away from work. He came out to the farm because I think he actually liked being around people who worked hard and knew the value of the dollar. Mike arrived at the farm one day when Dad had a crew of workers unloading hay wagons into the barn. The gas engine elevator was sending the bales up into the mow and the crew shut off the motor to take a break and to heckle Mike. He endured the expected banter, "Oh, you show up in a white shirt and tie when there is work to be done!" And, "Nothing like a city boy coming out to the farm!" Mike took off his tie, rolled up his sleeves and told the guys on the wagon to take a break. He started the motor, throttled up the speed, and proceeded to send bales into the mow almost end to end. The guys in the hay mow were buried in bales but they didn't dare tell Mike to slow down. They just tried to survive the onslaught until the wagon was empty.

The local rumor was that Bill Elsey was hooked up with men in Chicago that had, what do you say, questionable reputations. I vividly remember walking with Dad into Bill Elsey's service department, when I was 10 or 11 years old, to check on a vehicle we were having serviced. We witnessed multiple stations where men were reloading shotgun shells. There was a pile of bulk shot bags on the floor that was three feet deep and probably 12' X 14' square.

I doubt those shells were to be used by hunters. Another life lesson that Mike had mastered was that he always made sure that Bill Elsey's wife, Phylliss' car was washed, waxed, and full of gas. Happy Boss's wife, happy Boss, happy Mike. She drove a Cadillac and if we saw her in town, Dad always commented that her car was bright and shiny. Dad shared another story about Mike with me. One evening during family dinner, Mike came to our house to talk to Dad. Standing by the kitchen table he told Dad he was headed to Chicago and he asked if Dad wanted to ride along, he would enjoy the company. Dad thought there might be some trouble and told him as much. Mike opened his suit coat to expose a gun and said, "We won't have any trouble." Dad decided not to go to Chicago.

The 'First' Marilyn...

I believe you are finally dead when people no longer tell your story. The purpose of this chapter is to prevent my mother's finality by telling her story. My mother, quite possibly, lived the perfect life. She kept numerous friends from diapers to death. They were able to put aside family issues, politics, religion, children, husbands and life's drama and remain friends. She kept in touch constantly with her group of friends. She was a charter member of the 'Madison Township Hotline'. She was a rebel, organized to a fault, always helped people improve their lot, and continually studied in order to provide self-improvement.

I never saw her smoke cigarettes or drink alcohol. She even chose the grape juice on the outer edge of the tray during communion. Toward the end of her life, I had come to the realization that I had never heard her utter the words, "I'm sorry." I inquired to her about this, not sure how she would answer. She replied, after careful thought, "I don't think I have ever done anything that would cause me to say I'm sorry."

This was not arrogance; this was acknowledgement of a mistake-free life. I can't recall any action by her that would require an apology.

My mother, Marilyn Mae Beehler was born November 9th, 1924. The name Marilyn was not used at that time. I know of no one older than her with the name of Marilyn. Her dad, Adam Beehler, wanted to name her Mary and her mother, Emma, wanted to name her Lynn. A compromise resulted in Marilyn. Her close friends and family called her Mari, and her brother, Jim, called her Sis. My Mom and Dad deeply cared for each other.

They lived during a time when public displays of affection were rare, but their mutual teasing and non-verbal communication was proof of their affection. The quickest way to receive punishment from our father was to disrespect our mother. She was never the enforcer but there was always the fear of her telling Dad about our misbehaving.

The mere exercise of eating slowly could be perceived as a critique of Mom's cooking. After their wedding, on June 8th, 1947, they embarked on an 8257-mile honeymoon road trip in a 1940 something Oldsmobile traveling across the country. This trip was taken before the interstate road system was built. I am confident that this journey helped cement their partnership which lasted 63 years ending at my father's passing in 2010.

Mom and Dad's Wedding

Our mother was the original rebel. She played sports when few girls played sports. She played girls basketball for Madison School and backyard touch football with the neighborhood boys. She wore pants when girls weren't allowed to wear pants and rode a boy's bike. Her brother and she picked strawberries, at four cents a quart, to earn enough money to buy a bike. Jim didn't want to ride a girl's bike so they bought a Schwinn boys bike. Jim took their bike to Purdue as a freshman and sometime during the school year it was stolen. Jim said that he was on the lookout for that bike for two years and one day he finally spotted it in a bike rack. He said he 'stole it back' and then took it home. In 2016, the now 'antique' bike was stolen from our farm by a Madison Township theft ring. I never retrieved it. The sad part of this story was that the great grandfather of the leader of the theft ring and my grandfather, Adam, were neighbor farmers and friends in the 1920s.

My Dad was granted an agricultural exemption from the draft during WWII. Unbeknownst to him, a carload of local farmers drove to Indianapolis to testify on his behalf in front of the draft board.

They testified that if Herman went to war, most of their farms would be in jeopardy because Dad was the only young man in the area always helping everyone else farm. In the surrounding communities there was only a handful of young farmers that had exemptions. Duane Laidig, Roger Hahn, and Dick Phillips are the names that are in my memory. "We used to run around together" was their qualifying statement that I would hear from Dad. At the numerous rural youth square dances there would often be 200-300 young women and only 4 or 5 young men due to almost all of them being at war.

The guys might take a girl home and then they would return to the dance several times a night to repeat the process. Dad was 25 and Mom was 22 when they got married. They shared the same birthday.

During Mom's senior year of high school, she contracted what the Doctor called 'infectious arthritis'. She was the female lead in the school play and had to bow out due to her illness, just weeks before opening night. 60 years later she could still remember her lines. Her illness progressed at an irregular pace and she ignored the doctor's advice to not have children. She was very ill most of her life and subsequently was diagnosed with lupus, scleroderma, and rheumatoid arthritis.

My older sister, Michelle's main focus was studying. She was in school plays, played French horn in the band, a member of the debate team, NFL, NHS, DAR and was on the yearbook staff. This led her to be awarded Valedictorian of her class.

She received a teaching degree from Ball State University and graduated Magna cum laude. Michelle was an elementary school teacher at Concord East Side for 42 years. My father, my brother and I, all attended East Side Elementary. East Side School's 100-year anniversary will be celebrated in 2026. Dad went to first grade with the very first class in the new school in 1926.

Herman getting on the bus his first day of school

My activities included concert band, marching band, school plays, speech team, debate team, tennis, wrestling, college prep courses, class officer for three years, student council, honor society, newspaper reporter, yearbook, 4-H, Beef club, Jr. Leaders, Purdue Roundup, Presidential Classroom, and Boys State. I was in the group that was granted permission to see President Johnson in Dunlap, after the 1965 tornadoes. On May 2nd, 1968, I was standing in front of the Elkhart Post Office to listen to Robert Kennedy speak just weeks before his assassination.

All of these activities and opportunities were facilitated and encouraged by our parents, but mostly my mother. She was on us like white on rice. We were always doing projects, learning a new board game, playing card games or putting a puzzle or model car together. She once counted that she had made 27 trips to school in one week for the three of us, and we rode the bus to school!

I only have one record of her keeping a diary. She kept the diary on a preprinted 1965 journal. The journal had the days, dates, and lines pre-drawn for each of the 365 days. Even with her hands crippled from arthritis, Mom could write in artistic cursive. If you held the pages of the journal in your hand, and bent the journal to allow for acceleration, you could use your thumb as a governor and flip through the pages.

You would see no change in her writing from beginning to end. She also filled every line of each day, completely. Most diarists would run out of things to write about or have too much to write on any particular day. She filled every line, every day; no more, no less. I am quite certain she started out on January 1, 1965 with the determination to fill each day's entry only to the space allowed. She accomplished her goal.

Almost everyone in our neighborhood caught chickens for us. Catching chickens was relatively easy work, but dirty work. Dad always paid the catchers with a check at the end of each night's work. This practice of getting paid each night was an incentive to catch chickens for Dad. The amount was usually between $2.50 and $10.00, depending on the amount of work. C.C. and Pat Wisler were brothers that rode on our school bus. C.C. was one of my best friends since 1st grade.

Pat told me the following story about my Mom about 15 years ago. For some reason, Pat and C.C. had gotten off the bus at our house, they were planning on catching chickens that evening. Tetherball, basket-ball, and yard baseball were all on the agenda until the time arrived to catch chickens, which was dusk. Pat remembered that particular day was a Friday and Mom called us all in for supper. The Wisler's were Catholic and were called to eat fish on Fridays. The boys were wondering what would be on the menu. Pat said he never forgot my Mom's kindness and awareness when they found a supper of fish sticks waiting for them.

Mom made it a priority to know all of our friends, teachers, bus drivers, and school principals. She had a propensity to be on the phone. I think that was one of the ways she stayed up to date on all of the 'goings on' in the extended family and the neighborhood. Mom would routinely change the location of the furniture in the house just for the sake of changing and also to guarantee a clean house.

She always was on the lookout for anything 'new and improved'. A new restaurant, new recipe, new player on any team, or a new design, she wanted to be up to date on all the latest news. I have no idea when she had time to organize absolutely everything. Her clothes were color coordinated on their hangers in her closets and her antiques were all accompanied with information and their latest valuations.

Sorting through the attic after her passing, we found boxes of sent birthday cards and get-well cards organized in order of their receiving, lists in each box of names and addresses of who sent the cards, and check marked to note that a thank-you card had been sent. Scrapbooks and photo albums were dated, titled, and stacked in boxes.

One of our family's rules was that the last person to finish eating at the dinner table was rewarded or punished, depending on perspective, by getting the assignment to help Mom do dishes. We had a hundred-year-old farm sink with two chambers and a dish drying rack. I was a slow eater and spent many evenings rinsing dishes beside my Mom. We had a wooden stool with a red Cardinal painted on the top that I would stand on because I was too short to reach the sink. Today this stool supports our computer printer and it is right beside me as I write. Our time together at the sink helped me hone our shared sense of humor and cemented many positive traits of my character that she passed to me.

Mom and I could always count on each other to be each other's straight man and we always looked forward to sharing a joke, funny story, or just a valid anecdote. With her living in the main farmhouse even after Dad had passed, it allowed me easy access to check on her multiple times a day. An intended quick check, quite often, lasted hours. I could usually find her at the kitchen table, in the den, or sitting in her chair watching TV.

One day I came into the farmhouse and found her sitting in an unusual location. She was sitting in the chair in the dining room next to the hutch across the room from the telephone. "I've been waiting for you to stop in", she said. I thought to myself, "this can't be good."

She told me to sit down in the chair next to the telephone. My mind repeated my previous thought; "this can't be good." Once I was seated, she told me that she had reached a decision; "I have decided not to get remarried!" I broke out in laughter and said, "Please tell me I am the only one you have told this, because I am the only one who would think this is funny!" She said that I was, knowing I would laugh. After I regained my composure, I volleyed an expected comeback. "Do you have anyone in mind?", I asked. She returned the volley, "Well, that Bill King stops in while his wife is at the doctor, and sometimes I wonder." She was 88 years old at that time. I will never forget her slight grin and laughing eyes.

The afternoon before Dad's funeral, Mom was in the kitchen with Emilie, her granddaughter, Em's friend Toni, Beth and me. Em asked if she could get Mom anything and Mom replied that she usually had a glass of chocolate milk about this time of the day and she could make her a glass. Em got the milk out of the refrigerator and a tall glass out of the kitchen cupboard and began to pour the milk. Mom instructed her to leave plenty of room for the chocolate. When the milk was about 2 inches from the top of the glass, she was told that was enough milk. Em put the milk back in the frig and searched for the chocolate syrup. Not finding any in the frig, Mom told her that she keeps it in the cupboard to the left of the stove.

Emilie found the plastic container which was only part full and looked at the instructions that stated 'keep refrigerated after opening' and visually expressed her amazement! "Grandma, I think this is supposed to be refrigerated." She went to the glass of milk to add the chocolate syrup and asked Mom to say 'when'. As she squeezed in the chocolate, she repeatedly asked Mom, "Say when Grandma, say when." As it filled a one-inch void, Mom said "I think that is good." We burst into laughter as we realized we had found the key to a long life...unrefrigerated chocolate syrup in milk every afternoon. We still laugh at this story today.

One of the saddest statements I have ever heard in my life was uttered by Mom during her stay in the hospital after hip surgery. She had either broken a hip and fell, or fell and broke her hip, necessitating surgery. After surgery, she rehabbed at Hubbard Hill. About halfway through the rehabilitation Michelle and I noticed that she had made a turn for the worse. Rehab nurses and our brother missed the symptoms and were in the 'wait and see' camp. Michelle and I demanded an ambulance ride to the ER. Subsequent diagnosis confirmed that she had contracted C-dif. She was admitted and given IV antibiotics to counteract the infection. Her age, the surgery, and a poor immune system were all hurdles to her recovery.

Beth, Michelle, and I were in her hospital room at the lowest point, when Mom said, "I wish my mom was here." I had to leave the room to regain my composure and recover my emotions. I can't imagine a sadder statement from anyone, let alone someone in their 80s. She recovered from her hip surgery. In 2016, Mom tripped over one of her necessary area rugs and took a fall. A precautionary trip to the hospital revealed no broken bones but extensive internal cancer. We were all apprised of her prognosis for the coming weeks. She was fortunate to remain at home and the hospice pamphlet we were given seemed premature as she was still fairly self-sufficient. We all lived just minutes away and her phone and alert necklace provided alarms if needed. In just a few days more care was needed. Home nurses, home care and scheduled family assignments (for the most part) proved adequate. The hospice pamphlet soon became necessary reading.

I remember one particular paragraph of advice where it advised that the dying person, especially if they were a parent, wants reassurance that survivors are going to be O.K. I kept maneuvering my presence and practiced my line so that I could deliver it when there was no other nurses or family members were present. Heavily sedated with morphine, Mom spent her last days lying on her back in bed. An occasional sip of water and an occasional response were her only actions. She would respond if she felt one was necessary. My opportunity came. "Mom, you know we are going to be alright." After a pause, with her slight grin, she replied, "Only if there is enough money!" I told her if she was still cracking jokes, she was probably not going to die today. I miss being her straight man.

One of her few rules was, "don't call me during a Notre Dame women's basketball game." She was always perturbed when the Elkhart Truth would bury the results of the game in the back of the sports page. This would happen even when the Irish were nationally ranked. She was also upset that many of their games could only be heard on AM radio. She would extend her transistor radio's antenna with aluminum foil and listen to the game in the den. She was very proud that her cousin, Melissa Lechlitner, played for the Irish.

Mom invented pre-bagged sweet corn. When we moved our sweet corn sales to a wagon at the Grange Hall, it was a slow start. Art Lockwood, a neighbor, came down and helped us sell off of one of our hayracks. At first, the day consisted of story-telling and conversation and not much selling.

After a few days, sales started to pick up and at times we had a few customers at the same time. They would wait for a little while as we bagged their "Farmer's Dozens". Mom stopped by the wagon during one of those times when there were customers waiting and suggested that we bag some ahead so the customers didn't have to wait. Pre-bagged sweet corn was born. Before this, no markets or stores bagged corn ahead, it was always selected off a pile by the customer. Everyone thought they needed to check it, feel it, peel it back, before it was bagged. Our guarantee, our reputation and the "Farmer's Dozen" eliminated all of those issues. We got to the point where we had several wagonloads of pre-bagged corn ready for customers every day.

If you could boil down a summary of my mother's character to one word, it would be the word, 'fearless'. Every farm has quite a bit of road frontage, commonly referred to as 'roadside'. Whether it was fields, pasture, farmstead or wooded areas we tried to keep our roadsides picked up and free from trash. Before county dumps, landfills and trash pickup, the common practice was to take your trash out into the county and throw it along the road. Many hours and many a spring break were spent picking up the roadside trash along our farm's property. Can and bottle collections resulted from this exercise.

One particular story about trash pickup was an incident that occurred shortly after Mom and Dad were married. They were picking up trash along CR 14 just east of CR 15 along our wooded property on the north side of the road. Upon the inspection of a bag of trash, Mom found an envelope with the name and address of a doctor in town. They hatched a plot to return the trash or at the very least to see where he lived. Upon arrival, they went to the door and rang the doorbell and the door was opened. Much to my Dad's surprise, Mom burst in the door and scattered the trash all over the living room. She exclaimed, "We just wanted to return your trash!"

Years later I would repeat this same scene in the office of Irvine Shade and Door who had allowed their dumpster trash to blow into our field. Their factory lot literally looked like a landfill. I picked up all of their trash and deposited in the office of the plant manager. In the case of the doctor's trash, I want to believe that a third party was responsible for their trash disposal, but in any case, Mom definitely made her point. Her fearlessness fueled her rebellious nature.

We have an old family photo of a reunion/picnic from the 1930s. Mom's Aunt and Uncle had a summer home on Lake Wawasee where the reunion was held. There is close to one hundred family members in the photograph of all ages. I showed the picture to my children and challenged them to pick out which person was their grandmother. After examination and a clue that she would have been 10-years-old, they could not find her. I asked them again and reminded them that their grandma has always been a rebel. They pointed, correctly, to the only female wearing pants. This was a social no-no in the thirties. Anyone would also have to give credit to my grandparents for allowing her to buck the norms of the day.

Later in life, she shared some long-term memories with me. I believe that long-term memory is triggered in old age as a way to preserve oral history and pass on knowledge to future generations. She told me that one of her class-mates asked her to marry him before he left for WWII. She said, no. He never came back.

She also shared with me that my Dad had asked her to marry him during a trip to the Indiana State Fair. He had previously assured her that he would ask her during the daytime, that way she would know that he meant it. Maybe TMI? She was troubled late in life by just a few unanswered questions that were never settled to her satisfaction. I think she was looking forward to a time when these questions could be answered. Her oldest grandchild, Derek Blough, was killed in a tragic farm accident at a young age. The details were few, he was alone at the time.

She was always in search of the reason for his death. Mom was born and raised on a farm that her mom and dad were renting on Dogwood Road, St. Joseph County, Indiana. My memory is that they were renting from a relative. They were forced off the farm for reasons that are unknown to me.

At the age of 91, laying on her death bed, she told me that she couldn't understand why the landlord wouldn't allow her mom to dig up her peonies and take them with the move. "Those peonies were beautiful." In one of our philosophical conversations, I asked her if she ever knew anyone, that we would consider 'rich', that was worth a damn? She thought a while and answered, "No, I don't." I would love the chance to sit with her, share a story, or tell each other a joke. I take comfort in knowing that I had asked her almost every question while she was alive. She knew that I loved her and I knew that she loved me.

The 'First Marilyn', Marilyn Beehler Bullard

Dad, Herman, Herm...

I have struggled to find the words that could be put together that could describe the life of my father and best friend. Dad and I could communicate without speaking. One look between us could replace an entire conversation. He loved and respected our Mom and his wife of 63 years. He willingly taught those that wanted to learn. If I had to boil him down to one statement, it would be that he took great pleasure in seeing others succeed. I never heard him lie; he despised liars. He never cheated; he loathed people that cheated. He worked hard his entire life and enjoyed working.

Bruce Beehler, my 'favorite and best looking' cousin, in a taped interview asked Dad if he ever played sports? My Dad replied, "No, my hand fit a pitchfork better than a ball." By the time he was 23 years old he owned 2 tractors, a car, and an 80-acre farm...all paid for. His parents, Roy and Bernice, did not allow him to go to town by himself until he was 21. He could remember when he was very young, that one car a day would drive past our farm. An old man who lived in a shack close to present day Timberbrook mobile home park, drove by at 7:10 a.m. on the way to his job at the Federal Paper factory near present day Elkhart High School. 100 years later 30,000 cars pass by our farm daily.

Herman feeding his dog Pal and her pups. Circa 1926 Bullard Road in the background.

During his life, Dad farmed with horses and read computer printouts. He picked ear corn by hand and was one of the first farmers in the county to harvest and store shelled corn. In the 1980s he had the largest grain bin in the area, a 40,000-bushel Brock bin.

A few years later he erected another one the same size. At 5 years-old he had one cow to milk by hand. The cow's name was 'Beauty'. His dad always checked to make sure that she was milked dry. Dad was only 10 years-old when he went to the field for the first time, to rake hay for a neighbor with horses pulling the rake. He also planted 250 acres of corn in one day with an 8-row planter.

He milked cows by hand and lived to see cows milked by robots. He grew crops that were so poor that he had to decide if they were worth harvesting, and later, won many corn yield contests. When we started irrigating, he won the corn yield contest for several years in a row. These contests were usually won by farmers in the southern part of the county where the soil was heavier and more fertile.

Confronted with losing to someone that farmed blow sand, they created a non-irrigated classification and an irrigated classification. Dad was always trying to 'build a better mousetrap'. After noticing that the wheat grew greener, taller, and yielded larger heads when a cowpie was in close proximity he bought ammonium nitrate from Maumee, OH and drove our dual tandem grain truck and brought bulk fertilizer back to our farm. In the early 50s, during one such trip the truck broke down. He called home and convinced Mom to drive their Oldsmobile to where he was stranded. She towed the loaded truck home with their car.

Once back to the farm, Dad would transfer the bulk fertilizer to the back of a flatbed farm truck and scatter the fertilizer onto the wheat fields with a shovel while Mom drove the truck through the field. He also was one of the first farmers to side dress anhydrous ammonia on corn. He customed applied the nitrogen for other farmers as far away as Bremen, Indiana. His hired man, Johnny Hartman, would tow the 5-row applicator with our 450 IH tractor and Dad would follow with a nurse tank that would refill the applicator.

He built one of the first on-farm truck scales, owned one of the first two-way radio towers, designed and built an indoor grain dump pit, used a continuous flow corn dryer, and was one of the first farmers to bury irrigation pipe. In 1985, he was awarded the Indiana Prairie Farmer 'Master Farmer' designation.

When we started raising produce, he was more than willing to tackle any new idea or method that I proposed. Many area and statewide firsts included staked tomatoes and peppers, mulching in between produce rows by rolling out rye straw round bales, using drip irrigation, planting cover crops, machine harvesting sweet corn, row covering green beans, using plastic mulch, raising pumpkins, fall hayrides, night hayrides, corn mazes, on-farm petting area, selling corn fodder shocks, delivering fall displays, raising Indian corn, straw tunnels, Farmer's Dozen sweet corn, and pre-bagged sweet corn.

We purchased the first surrogate that was pregnant with a purebred Angus embryo in the history of the Angus breed. We transplanted embryos for ourselves and commercially for others, we were part owners of the record selling Angus bull of the Indiana Angus Futurity and raised and sold the record selling Angus female. We were the first to market a bull's semen through sending VHS tapes to prospective customers. For context, this was before cell phones, the internet, and social media. We used coupons and a newsletter to help market our Bullard Farms Sweet Corn.

Herman and Kurt Bullard circa 1990

Bullard Farms Market held an annual Sweet Corn Festival where we provided FREE, all-you-can-eat grilled corn. This was such a popular summer event that we needed to recruit the mounted Bristol Police unit to help control traffic. One of our 'satellite' locations was the Shipshewana Flea Market where we sold our corn in the produce lane for ten summers. There were many vendors reselling sweet corn that they had bought. Our stand was one of the few that sold fresh corn that we had raised. Our corn was always priced higher than the other vendors constantly proving "you get what you pay for."

One week during peak season I decided to initiate "Corn Wars!" The flea market was held on Tuesdays and Wednesdays. On a Tuesday morning in August, War was declared! We had extra workers and wagonloads of corn ready for battle. We lowered our price in order to be the cheapest on the produce isle. As the other vendors lowered their price we countered. By the end of the day, a Farmer's Dozen was 50 cents. By the time we got back to the farm to bring another wagon we would receive word the wagon at the market was already sold out. We even sold IOU corn tickets and would redeem them once our wagon got back to the Flea Market. We sold 10 wagonloads that day. The profit was made the next day when we raised our price back to normal and easily sold our fresh corn because the other vendors had day-old corn left from the previous day that was hard to sell. The legend of the 'Corn Wars' was the topic of many restaurants' farmer-table discussions.

Bullard Farms Sweet Corn wagon

1991 was the year our farm turned 100-years-old. My great-grandfather, Phillip Aurelius Bullard, signed the deed on November 19, 1891. Dad had been thinking about having a Centennial Celebration for years and we planned the event. The corner field was sown to a hay mix, entertainment was scheduled, a large tent ordered, invitations were sent, flowers were planted and several farm buildings were painted.

Volunteers helped with parking, serving the food and cooking. The date, June 23rd was chosen, with moon cycles taken into consideration, and the weather turned out to be perfect. The Centennial Celebration was a huge success. Mom, of course, chronicled everything in photo albums and scrapbooks including pictures and thank you cards. It was a great day in the history of the farm.

During his life, Dad survived a heart attack and subsequent bypass surgery, and a knee replacement that needed to be redone after the first one failed. He had several back issues that, sometimes, required bed rest for weeks. With the help of our hired men, the chores were done and the irrigation kept running during those times.

In 1972, Mom and Dad planned a trip to Hawaii to celebrate their 25th wedding anniversary. Our corn crop was outstanding and instead of being 'knee high by the fourth of July', it was 6-8 feet tall and almost tasseling. While they were gone it got cold enough to frost the top portion of the entire crop. The top third of the plants turned brown after a few days. The uncertainty of the crop was discussed the entire season. After studying all of the information available, we decided to let the crop run its course. After harvest, by comparing other fields, we determined that the yield had not been reduced by the frost.

Our shop was the heart of our farm. At one time we had three different areas serve as a shop. Each serving a different purpose, either fabrication, repair or storage of tools. In the 1970's, we decided to consolidate them into one shop by converting a building that was originally built for machinery storage. It also had an area to shell ear corn and store ear corn. Benches and parts bins were built. The parts bins were placed in the narrow ear corn crib along the north wall. We organized the parts bins by seasons to make it easier to locate a particular part. We used an old Dowagiac wood stove for heating. The shop had many tables, boxes and cabinets filled with bolts, nuts, and screws. We bought many bolts and nuts from farm auctions. Dad used to say, "we have more bolts and nuts than the hardware store."

We had an anvil mounted on a large oak stump that was used daily to break, shape, bend, and repair all kinds of materials and parts. I was disappointed when Dad told me that he planned on giving the farm anvil to my brother. I expressed my surprise due to my brother's rare use of the anvil. Dad replied, "Oh, you will find one to replace it someday." I assumed that he meant I would buy another one at another farm auction and mount it on the barren oak stump. After Dad had passed, I was cleaning, sweeping, and organizing the shop when I found 'it'. Placed under one of the built-in benches, behind the storage bins, was a perfect large anvil. I have no idea how or when it was placed there, but I recalled his words and smiled. The anvil is being used today to build Janus Motorcycles in Goshen, Indiana. In June of 2010, Dad started having some mini strokes that affected his balance, speech and eyesight.

The doctor admitted him to the hospital to run tests and try to determine the location of the clot producing the strokes. About 10:00 p.m., June 15, 2010 I was sitting in our living room with Beth watching the news and I told her I was going to run in to the hospital to see Dad. When I got to his room, he was asleep but was soon awakened by the usual hospital noise. He was glad to see me and said, "Tell me something I don't know." This was a metaphor for his life, always curious. Always wanting to learn. At 2:30 the next morning I got the call that his heart had stopped and they were unable to revive him. He used to say, "my body is wearing out." He was 88-years-old. He was born and lived in the same house his entire life.

Toward the end of Dad's life, Michelle had given him a spiral notebook and asked him to write down some memories and advice. Michelle was under the impression that he never accomplished her request. They weren't written in the spiral notebook that she had given him. His notes were written on a pad that was in a box in his office that I was given, marked 'for Kurt'.

'Hermanisms' are as follows:

"Don't worry about the mules, load the wagon!"

"Serve the good wine first"

"If you want to sell something good, make it easy to buy it"

"Never chase a fad"

"Greed will gobble up our soul, unless we say 'No'"

"Winners never cheat"

"Bankers are difficult to deal with"

"People that have made their money are not good on a committee"

"The hungry and the homeless don't vote"

"He was born on second base" (somebody not very good)

"Bankers do not take risks knowingly, if there is a risk, they would not take it"

"I worried more in the 1980's about going broke than I have about my cancer for the last 13 years, it is all about attitude. I can, I will beat it."

"In life, you lose more than you win, it keeps you humble"

"today's peacock is tomorrow's feather duster"

"don't get in a fight you can't win"

"I have no corp. ladder to climb, just want to do a good job"

"How many angels can dance on the head of a pin?"

"Plagiarism is OK if the other person is quoting you"

"Losers don't get any cigars"

"I can hear you getting fat"

"It takes a crook to know one, they think alike"

"If we are good to the Mexican immigrants, they might help us fight a war"

"I don't claim to be misunderstood"

"I don't need to salute you"

"You don't learn anything from somebody that always agrees with you"

"When you get mad, you expose your weakness"

"Leaders in a war do not draw"

"When somebody is digging a hole, let them dig"

"If you don't want to talk about your mistakes, don't worry, I will"

"I don't need an editor to edit the truth"

"Never underestimate an opponent"

"To look back in time is wasted by not looking forward"

"I think Abe L. would be proud of Obama, not because he is a candidate, but because he could be."

"Which one of these men would NOT be in favor of Obama? 1. Abe L. 2. Tom Jefferson 3. Or Martin L. King? Ans. None"

"Which one don't you like? 1. Dec. of Indep. 2. Emancipation Proclamation 3. I have a dream?"

"I don't see how a preacher could be anything but a democrat"

"It's better to lose an election than lose your principles"

"Defense is fought best with the truth"

"Do you have a #2 pencil to write this down?"

"Jefferson said, 'a majority of one, is just as powerful as a unanimous vote'."

"I think the answer to the race problem is people will become 'grey'."

"I will never give up, no matter what!"

"Come hell and high water"

"I don't want to have a beer with you, but I would like to be able to afford one"

"When simple becomes really simple, it becomes Grand! (life)"

"When math is difficult, make it simpler"

"I love Mari"

"Don't argue over the truth but for the truth"

"The 'elite' have a diff. idea about feeding the poor, They are not in support of it because They were never hungry."

"If you don't agree with me that's OK, but I am not sitting in the back of the bus"

"Voters in Va. And No. C that voted for Hillary, grandfathers owned slaves and fought in the Civil War"

There is no such thing as a nobody, but you are close"

"Don't go along just to get along"

"News and noise can be similar or opposite"

"Work solves a lot of problems"

"Always give your speech after the other guy"

"What is a Polly Annie? A push over"

"I might make you mad, but 'I will not get mad'. I want to be above that"

"What are the three faces of Eve?"

"Has any first time President ever been ready to be pres.?"

"When you Plow and you hit a buried stone, experience don't help muck because no 2 are the same. Only common sense will help"

"You have to stay on the offensive or it won't be effective or the other politicians will whip you"

"Watch me make sausage of your ideas"

"That dog won't hunt"

"I never doubted that I would be successful"

"Even a broken clock is right 2X a day. (you can't be wrong all the time)

"don't check your watch during a debate or an argument"

"Be learry of people bearing gifts is you 'think' they are looking for a favor"

"Don't follow the guy that is leaving the ship."

"He will suffer from whiplash" (said the wrong thing)

"Start the Buzz and stir it up"

"Keep things simple"

"You don't need to memorize a speech if you have it in your heart"

"No education is the 2nd kick of the jackass"

"You don't need to tell me how honest you are, someone else will"

"Some things are always wrong; somethings are always right. Amen"

"I am my father's son"

"Try to disagree and not be disagreeable"

"Always dance with the boy that brought you"

"I will carry your bags, but I would like to be heard"

"Obama is my man, 2-4-08"

"You don't need a college degree to have a PHD in life"

"It took his tent down"

"Never be the last to go home"

"This is so bad it makes my teeth hurt"

"Your opinion is toxic to me"

"They don't give PHDs for common sense"

"I don't want anybody to kiss up to me to win their point of view"

"Obama, yes I can"

"I don't like to be around people that are something they ain't"

"I don't give up till last dog dies"

"If your opponent is getting beat up verbally, stay out and let other people do the dirty work"

"Go rent a mule so you hitch up to another jackass, you will make a good team"

"You should probably check the water you are drinking"

"Did you write the literacy questionnaire so I cannot give my opinion?"

"I think I want people elected to office that are new in politics, they don't want people that are warpt by being in office."

"Big news stories get on the front page, above the fold"

"Big money warps politicians"

"Trust takes time"

"Do you think your vision for this country is different than mine?"

"If you want to be content with your life, you have to be satisfied with what you got, you will feel real good. HLB"

"There is no zealot like a convert"

"The lies will fall from the weight of the truth"

"it's an election, not a coronation"

"Never ask for big donations, no more than 5-dollar bill, send back the rest"

"If you want to strengthen your faith, be a farmer"

"God is a 'God of Passion', and he expects us to do the same"

"With God's help, I can do anything"

"It is good to be a farmer, then you will under estimate me!!"

"a farmer has more experience than any occupation on earth"

"Always take the Hi Road"

"Are you a snake oil salesman?"

"de-fang the snake? You can with the truth."

"Did you lose one of your lenses out your glasses? You are only seeing ½ way"

"I want to die broke and it may be a balancing act to make sure I have enough, and you are not on my list of how to tip the scales...I decide."

"Voters-boots on the ground"

"Hang a lantern on your problem" Bob Kennedy

"Arguments are won with facts and truth"

"Not only do I want to see your diploma, I want to see your grade point ave."

"The government has to tell the Truth!"

"Stick to your principles if you are right, but always admit it if you find out you were wrong"

"Somebody who can't make up their mind 'won't go to the altar'"

"Good words...shucks and Gosh"

"I like people that got guts to stick to their opinion"

"Only Liberals build"

"I will write my own pedigree"

"It don't make any difference how far you go but if you are going forward"

"Gold does not buy salvation"

"Never give the media a bad word. Because they won't help you at all"

"I am a liberal because conserve. do not help people conserve. are only for the rich and big money."

"IKE was a conservative and a whiskey drinking Republican, Democrats drink beer."

"If it is better than it looks, they will talk. If it is worse than it looks, they won't talk. Tiger Woods Nov. 30, 09"

"You don't need a script to tell the truth."

"Live like you are going to live forever then you will be ready to die."

"Never give up"

"I hope and pray that I live the way HE wants me to"

"Mother Nature makes the rules in a storm and politics"

"I want to be doing something constructive"

"On the farm, there is always another story problem right around the corner"

I am my father's son, KLB

The 13 acres...

This field, that we called the '13 acres', was located on the southeast corner of CR 14 and CR 17. Roy, my grandfather, received it as part of the "dowry" when he married my grandmother, Bernice Pollack. The soil was so poor that he just pastured the dairy cows on it between milkings, rather attempt to raise a crop. Dad told me that they never had a gate on the field where the cows entered and exited. Their dog, Pal, would take the cows down to the pasture and then run back to the farm and lay in the yard, on watch. If a cow came up to the opening sometimes Pal only needed to stand up and the cow would know to back away from the opening. If a cow would challenge Pal's authority, she would race down to the corner to remind the cow who was in charge. When Dad first started farming on his own, he was determined to make the barren 13 acres productive. He explained that he sowed rye in the fall and plowed down the "green manure" crop in the late spring the next year.

The rye was usually too tall to be plowed under; he would have to drag a wire behind each moldboard to force the tall rye to fold under the freshly plowed soil. After the rye was plowed under, he sowed sudan grass in late June and plowed that down in the fall and followed with rye again. He plowed that crop under the following spring. That year the field produced a crop that he could harvest. We removed several fence rows and trees on the farm to allow for bigger equipment and to gain acres. The corner 13 acres and adjoining fields were combined to form a 27-acre field. In the middle of the field stood a huge red oak tree that provided many truckloads of firewood. Many weeks of burning tires and diesel fuel finally burnt out the stump. If there was a spare moment, we would take another tire to the oak stump. Farmers, to this day, are historically uneducated about their contributions to damaging the environment.

When the county rebuilt the road between our farms, we installed a culvert to enable us to slide irrigation pipe from the west to the east side of CR 17. This gave us the ability expand our irrigated acreage. Those fields on the east side of CR 17 grew field corn, sweet corn and Indian corn, pumpkins, cantaloupe, green beans, and peppers. We planted pie pumpkins, gourds, and cantaloupe in one of the small fields up by the barn one season in the mid-90's. Erin Payne and I were in that patch harvesting when a bee launched out of the vines and stung me just below the left eye. It felt like I had been hit by a professional boxer. I immediately covered my nose and mouth to keep the other bees from attacking and ran from the field. My resulting black eye marked the point of the attack. The bees were on high alert for weeks, preventing me from entering the patch. I found out the beekeeper, that I had rented the hives from, had introduced some Africanized bees to his colony that are notoriously aggressive. I changed my beekeeper the next season.

Another incident happened on the 13 acres involving goose hunters. For about 20 years in the 80's and 90's our farm was in the path of migrating Canadian geese. As a good farming practice, we planted rye as a cover crop after we harvested our sweet corn patches. The combination of emerging rye shoots and left-over sweet corn provided a buffet for the geese. We always welcomed their arrival, because they scared away the blackbirds and starlings that were experts at damaging the ready-to-harvest sweet corn. Groups of geese would arrive to our fields the entire day and would leave in the same groups at dusk. They would fly to nearby lakes and ponds where they would overnight.

I was driving back to the farm one mid-afternoon with my young son, Peter, when I noticed the entire field of geese take flight in unison. As we came closer to the field, I noticed two hunters carrying geese and they were walking towards a van parked along CR 14 across from the duplexes next to our house. I pulled up in back of the van and radioed for family backup. I walked toward the hunters and confronted them about their trespass. I instructed them to drop the geese and leave. They refused. Don Boyer, the owner of the duplexes, came from across the road. He was in one of the duplexes, with his grandson, when he heard the gunshots. Don was extremely agitated. I told him to call the sheriff, and he replied that he already did. This response prompted the hunters to throw the geese into their van through the sliding side door, get in and prepare to leave. I moved to the back of their van and proceeded to kick a large dent in the door. They stopped and got out holding their guns. I remember Peter crying in the cab of my truck, rightfully scared.

About this time, Deputy Brown pulled up in his sheriff's car and a few more sheriff deputies arrived shortly after. Deputy Brown and his wife had rented one of Dad's rental houses when they were first married.

My Dad arrived soon after the deputies and when he pulled up, all the deputies, in unison, said, "Hi, Herm!" The hunters had to know that their situation was going from bad to worse very quickly. Deputy Brown opened the side door of their van to discover that one goose was still alive. His demeanor shifted gears and the hunters were detained to the hood of a vehicle, hand-cuffed and escorted to the sheriff cars. The hunters had no driver's license, no hunting license, they lived in Michigan, which meant they crossed state lines and committed a crime. Their van was impounded and then they had the nerve to ask about the damage that I had caused to their van. Deputy Brown told them that I was protecting my property from theft.

Pine Creek...

Pine Creek didn't run through our farm but it divided a field that I farmed for 42 years. In 1980 it was part of the Ralph Dull estate and we decided that particular parcel was too expensive to buy. It was priced at $2400 per acre. 40 years later, it is valued at $80,000 per acre. Erv Gilder, a local real estate broker, thought he could find someone to buy those parcels from the estate and agree to allow me to farm the land. I bought an Ag Rain irrigation traveler and a John Deere Power unit with a pump and installed 6" underground pipe to irrigate the crops along 7 irrigation lanes. I had a supply pond dug to the side of the creek to comply with the rule preventing the withdrawal of water directly from a stream.

Each year was a battle to keep the traveler working properly and to provide enough water to the pond to keep the pump primed. The two fields produced some outstanding crops over the years. The source of Pine Creek's north branch was a short hand-dug ditch on the east side of CR 35 just south of CR 22. The south branch sourced just west of CR 35 on the south side of CR 20. These two branches joined and flowed west, northwest, and sometimes due north all the way to the St. Joseph River west of CR17. I have a copyrighted photograph, dated 1904, of the mouth of Pine Creek as it flowed into the river. Eudora Mitchel Light made this notation on the back of the framed picture. 'Pine Creek at any old house on Jackson St. Looking north from the old wood bridge'. Sections of Pine Creek and the St. Joseph River flow north. Very few bodies of water flow north in the entire country. I have long-wanted to float Pine Creek from it's beginning to the river. My time is running out to get this feat accomplished. When we were young, we would ride our bikes to the creek. We spent hours building sand dams and canals and caught minnows under the CR 14 bridge.

One of the area's tragedies, connected with Pine Creek, involved Arbor Lakes apartment development and the construction of the US 20 bypass. The apartment complex was built on land that was basically stolen from a blind, widow for $900 per acre by a real estate broker. A lake was dug to provide fill for the construction of the apartments and to provide a retention area for runoff. When the bypass was built, sand was excavated from the bottom of the lake and sold to the road contractor.

When all of the sand that was available had been extracted, the lake was lowered by pumping the water to Pine Creek via a 2' pipe along the mile course from the lake to the creek. The result provided the opportunity for the complex owner to sell more fill for the road construction. The water that was pumped contained sediment and the process added 8" of yellow sand to the bottom of the creek from US 20 to the river. No permits were obtained from any regulatory agencies. IDEM, DNR, Army Corps of Engineers, County, State... nothing. This was corroborated to me by the County Surveyor when I inquired.

The damage was done before anything could be done to stop it.

The creek was not the only thing that got filled, pockets of developers and politicians were also filled. Ralph Dull envisioned in the 30's that Pine Creek would someday be dammed every 80 rods to enable farmers to irrigate and regulate the flow of the creek. 100 years later the Creek is being classified in stages to allow for commercial development, not for farming. In the 80's, there were at least ten farmers irrigating out of the creek, today, maybe one. During dry summers, the creek would almost cease to flow. I would pray for rain or at least pray that it would rain somewhere upstream, to allow the creek to flow. There were rumors that a farmer dammed the creek with round bales of hay to hold back the flow and allow him to irrigate. I think those were just rumors.

Floyd Swinehart owned our farm on the east side of CR 17 in the 30's. Dad told me that Floyd was extremely particular when it came to the care of his Jersey milk cows. He would throw the silage down from the silo in the evening and cover the pile with blankets in the winter to prevent the frosty feed from damaging the stomachs of the cows. Floyd always had a bottle of whiskey hidden behind the pile of used baler twine hanging on a nail on the barn wall. He, like most all farmers, struggled to keep his farm during the depression. The bank foreclosed on his farm weeks before WWII broke out. Prices rose substantially during the war and Floyd would have made it if the bank would have given him just a little more time. The neighborhood story was that one of the banker's relatives bought the farm from the bank and rented it back to Floyd. I am uncertain of when Dad bought that farm.

Another neighborhood story involved Floyd's mother when she was a little girl, in the mid 1800's. The story was told that she wandered to the east of the farm to play in Pine Creek. Upon finding a birch bark canoe, she ran yelling and screaming back home scared of a possible encounter with an Indian. Imagine the historical significance, if someone had retrieved the canoe and stuck it up in the barn rafters. Pine Creek was part of a portage between the Elkhart River and the St. Joseph River which traversed to Lake Michigan. This passage is likely the reason for the canoe, and the source of plentiful arrowheads that we found in the fields bordering this path.

In the 80's Pine Creek was scheduled to be dug out by the County Drainage Board. The contractor dug the entire creek in the opposite direction that it should have been dug. When his progress was directly east of the Swinehart farm, I walked back to watch the excavation. The operator yelled from his seat, "Watch this!" The backhoe was sitting in the creek and he lowered the entire length of the excavator arm into the creek-bed without resistance. Quicksand! If he had not discovered this phenomenon his entire machine might have been swallowed. He climbed the backhoe up the bank and detoured the quicksand. This was the second spot of quicksand that I was aware of in my lifetime. We lost a cow in quicksand on a pasture located north of US 20 off CR 33 on the Nihart farm.

Irrigating the fields, we called Pine Creek East and Pine Creek West, was always a challenge of tangled cables, loss of water pressure, the breaking of the many roller chains on the traveler or a leak in a hose. The battle against these gremlins demanded extra time and effort. My dog, Lucy, was my constant companion. She would wander the fields and irrigation lanes while I was laboring moving the irrigation unit or starting the pump. Mom and Dad pulled into the Pine Creek main lane one day, and encountered Lucy standing in the middle of the lane. Mom rolled her window down and asked her, "Where's Kurt?" Lucy turned and ran down the lane to where I was working with Mom and Dad following her in their car. Mom was always proud of how smart

Lucy was and told this story many times.

An inhabitant of the Pine Creek area was a mammoth white-tail buck. In the fall his 12-14-point rack would be so heavy that he would bob his head as he walked along the creek or in the irrigation lanes. We would see him frequently during the foggy, fall mornings walking just ahead of Harley's sweet corn picker. The hunters, that didn't have permission to hunt, would tell stories of their encounters with the elusive deer. We would overhear their stories of the buck that had hoof prints as 'big as a cow's'. We never gave him another name besides "The Buck". In my mind he is still roaming Pine Creek.

Chapter Six

BACK TO THE FARM

Witty, Wise, Wild, Wonderful Workers...

The farm had dozens of people that worked for, and with us. That total increased dramatically when we started raising produce. I am certain that worker stories could fill the pages of another book on their own. Many of those have been forgotten or are unknown to me. I have chosen the following stories to include in this attempt.

Jerry Yoder was a hired man that worked for Dad in the 1960s. He could drive anything. I remember him to be very athletic and he moved with ease. He was good at playing basketball and eagerly taught me the necessary skills for me to be good at the game. He helped me choose the left elbow of the lane as my favorite shot. He challenged me to shoot

500 shots a day from that spot. Harry Myers was another hired man that left a strong imprint on my memory. Harry thrived on following the daily schedule that was necessary to complete the chicken chores. Walking each chicken house, checking feeders, cleaning waters were twice daily chores. You could set your watch on his arrival and the amount of time it took for him to complete the chores.

Farming and moving irrigation pipe filled up the rest of his hours at the farm. Bill Wutrich, Dean Shue, Larry Minarik, James Eastman, and Johnny Hartman were also hired men that I remember working for Dad. When we started raising sweet corn and produce, Art Lockwood, Paul Weaver, Al Renn, and Dick Roske, all helped us sell corn. Countless 'English' and 'Amish' kids worked on our farm.

The Nic Hernandez family, notably Nic and his children Sarita and Raf, helped pick acres of green beans. Picking green beans competed with pitching manure by hand, baling oat straw, and milking cows by hand, for the title of 'Worst Farm Job'. Working in the hot sun, moving along the row at a snail's pace, and back aching positions all describe the work environment. A person could pick green beans for an hour, move only 10 feet down the row, and barely fill a five-gallon bucket with beans. I always wanted to be familiar with any task that I charged any of my employees with doing. After my first day of picking beans, I could hardly move. I asked Nic about my pain and he told me, "Oh, that will go away in a few days." Nic became my friend. We cleared fencerows, cut wood, picked pumpkins, and tied Indian corn into bundles by the hundreds; not as boss-worker but as friends.

The Hernandez family was not the only family that had numerous members, if not their entire families, work for us. The McGinn, Steede, Millers, Yoders, Mast, Bontragers, Law, Clark, Stahly, Adamson, Wagler, Nihart, Shupert, Adcock, Spangle, Graber, Sweet and Doering families all helped us keep our farm successful. A handful of these workers were members, of what I called, my 'first string'. These were the ones that worked the entire day and sometimes seven days a week. I remember a few weekly time sheets that recorded over 100 hours. Tara Steede, Larry Miller, Gene Herschberger, Angie and Elizabeth Adamson, and Erin Payne were all members of my 'first string'.

Delivering wagons, loading wagons with produce for the satellite locations, mowing yards, painting signs, repairing fence and buildings, sweeping sorting floors, feeding cows, washing vehicles, planting and harvesting pumpkins and other produce, binding corn shocks, tying Indian corn, and watching our kids were all jobs on their list. We had great workers. I must have been a terrible boss, because the common thing they all say when I see them today, is that they had a lot of fun working at Bullard Farms.

Erin Payne...

Erin worked for me for 8 years; during high school, college and after. She graduated from the University of Vermont in Sustainable Agriculture. Erin was working on the farm on September 11, 2001. When we heard the news, we ran to the farmhouse kitchen and watched, on Mom's small television, as the plane flew into the second tower.

It was of some comfort to watch that tragedy with someone rather than be alone. Erin accomplished every job or task that she was assigned and many times she assigned me tasks. She usually drove the sweet corn wagon the dozen, or so, miles to Mrs. Zimmerman's farm in Wakarusa. Maggie Zimmerman sold our corn for 20 years. You could set your clock on the amount of time it took Erin to make the trip delivering the sweet corn. My rule for the people that delivered corn was that they had to pay their own speeding tickets. One day it took longer than usual for

Erin to return, and I started to worry.

After considerable time had passed, she arrived back to the farm, stopped where I was standing, and tossed me a ticket. She said, "You are paying this one!" She had been pulled over on the bypass for an unknown reason. The officer was certain there was some violation because a farm wagon was being towed 50-55 miles per hour. She was not happy that he sat in his car for 30 minutes trying to figure out what regulation she had violated. Wasted time, by anyone, was not appreciated. The violation that he decided upon was lack of registration for the wagon.

We had a few wagons that could travel straight at that speed and those were always the ones that were loaded to go to Mrs. Z. Her night-court date ended up being the night before she was to leave to go back to school. She asked if I would go with her for the hearing. We were the only middle-class white people seated in the courtroom. No judgement, just fact.

The cases were called by alphabetical order; therefore we had some time before they got to the Ps. While we were waiting, one violator reentered the courtroom after his case had been adjudicated. He complained to the judge about an extra $25 charge. The judge informed him that the arresting officer noted that he was rude, and in his court, rudeness costs $25. I had a copy of the Polk book for evidence that stated 'implements of husbandry shall be exempt from registration'.

A farm wagon loaded with sweet corn was certainly an implement of husbandry. The wagon had reflectors and safety chains and we were ready to plead 'not guilty'. When she was called to the front, the judge asked her if she was ready to leave for school? Puzzled, she answered that she was leaving tomorrow. He wished her good luck and entered her plea of not guilty. The bailiff escorted us to the hallway where we were to wait to talk to the public defender. A short time later the bailiff came out to the hall and said, "Erin Payne, case dismissed."

I took Erin home and she called me later to tell me that the Judge's daughter was also attending the University of Vermont. What are the chances of that? Erin's dad was connected in Elkhart and I don't know if he had a role in the dismissal. A mantra was proven again; "It's not what you know, but who you know." Erin was smart, ambitious, and a hard worker. Beth and I are fortunate and blessed to call her a friend.

The Obama Barn...

In April of 2008, I received a phone call from Rohan Patel, a senior advisor to, then presidential candidate, Barack Obama. They were looking for a farm location to hold an agriculture themed town hall. Rohan's parents lived in nearby Goshen, Indiana and he remembered our farm because he had come to our pumpkin patch on a field trip when he was in first grade. Senior advisor?

He said he didn't know if I was a Democrat, possibly a Hillary supporter, or an Obama supporter, or even if we would be interested in hosting a town hall. I answered, "yes, no, yes, yes." I had to remind him of the questions that he had just asked. The next day two staffers came to our farm and spent four hours in our farm's driveway emailing, conducting conference calls, taking pictures of the location and touring the farm.

Reggie Love was one of the staffers. I found out later that he was Barack's right-hand man and friend. They left telling me that they would let me know later that evening. At that time, I was the secretary for the Elkhart County Democratic Party and we were having a Central Committee meeting that evening. During the meeting I received the call from the Obama campaign informing me, that due to logistics, they decided to hold the town hall at neighboring St. Joseph County fairgrounds instead of our farm.

They proceeded to ask me if I would introduce Barack at that town-hall! I hesitated for a minute to ask the committee if they thought I could do this. They said sure and I accepted the invitation.

Adora Andy called me the following day with the details, and in accordance with my DNA, I had some questions! A year after hurricane Katrina, I had worked with Ken Wetzel, rebuilding neighborhood homes. Ken was awarded the "Volunteer of the Year" award from George W. Bush when he arrived in New Orleans to view the damage. Ken told me that he was instructed what color of shirt and pants to wear and how many times to roll up the sleeves of his shirt. Having this knowledge of potential protocols, I asked Ms. Andy, "what I should wear?" She replied that decision was up to me. I asked, "what should I say, was there a script?" She again told me that it was entirely up to me; a total green light.

Dozens of news outlets from all over the country and the world would be covering the town hall and they trusted me to introduce, potentially and ultimately, the President of the United States. The townhall was scheduled for Wednesday, April 30, 2008. Beth and I arrived at the fairgrounds, parked and entered the building where the town hall was to be held. Straw bales were placed in a large circle for the guests' seating surrounded by film crews. Beth was escorted to her straw bale and I was led to another building to wait for Barack.

He was in the process of filming David Letterman's Top Ten for the next night's Late Night episode. When he came out from the filming, I was introduced to him and we talked on the way to the event building. After I introduced him, he shared his vision for renewable energy, the importance for the country to invest in rural America, and the invaluable contribution that agriculture and farmers provide to the country and the world. As he had done many times, after his speech, he answered questions and toured the room signing autographs and taking selfies with guests. When he got around the straw circle to Beth and I, he leaned in and informed me that I had, "married up!" I responded, "So did you!" He countered, "I know!"

Candidate Barack Obama, Beth and Kurt Bullard

Four days later, on Sunday about noon, my friend Brent Curry called me and said, "He is on Bank Street!" In 2008, 'He' referred to Barack Obama. Elkhart, Indiana was the white-hot center of unemployment that was caused by Bush's failed policies and Barack came to our area several times to engage our community, as it was experiencing 22% unemployment. When I got to Bank Street, the line to meet him was blocks long. I soon found Reggie Love and other staffers that I had met just days previous. I wondered if I should get in line but was nervous about an awkward interaction that could result. He had met thousands of people since Wednesday and he couldn't possibly remember my introduction and certainly not my name. I was wrong. Reggie encouraged me to get in line and when Barack got within 20 feet or so, he looked up and exclaimed, "Kurt! I'll be there in just a few." He shook my hand and told me again how much he appreciated my help. I could barely speak. Since that time, I have heard other stories of his ability to remember names and events, sometimes for months. I was also fortunate to attend an NPR hosted event at Elkhart's Lerner Theatre on June 1st, 2016 at which President Obama held a question-and-answer townhall.

Back to the Obama Barn. In August, 2008 I got another call from Washington D.C., on a Sunday, from a volunteer on the Obama campaign inquiring if we would participate in a rural promotion, that was started in Ohio, called 'Obama Barns'? She had been told that we had a barn with high visibility on a busy road. I immediately agreed. She asked when we could possibly have it painted; I told her that we could have it painted by Friday.

Dad paid for the paint and Mom gave her approval because the barn was in her trust. I borrowed Steve Rumfelt's scaffold for the 'Big Machine' and repainted the barn roof white. My, quickly gathered, committee decided the design should copy an Obama bumper sticker 'Obama 08' including the rainbow/sunrise, red, white and blue logo. Dwight Fish took the bumper sticker to Staples and had a transparency made and Dave Geyer let us use his overhead projector to display the image on the barn at night.

We outlined the projected image with a sharpie, dotting the borders of the design to be painted the next few days. The word Obama and the

08 were two different shades of blue. The pantone color description of the word 'Obama' was 'Dignity Blue'. The project had the desired publicity outcome; news stories, television spots, and controversy followed. I invited all of those that helped on the project to sign one of the barn doors with a large magic marker and 32 signatures were realized. Thanks to all that helped. A special shout out to Zanzer Anderson and Ruth Trinkley, who endured 99-degree temperatures to paint the majority of the masterpiece.

Our Obama Barn

Johnny Cash and June Carter Cash...

This story took place outside the 2-mile radius from our farm, but it involves our Bullard Farms Sweet Corn, Johnny Cash and June Carter Cash, therefore it is a worthy story to include. The 'Ribeye Tent' at the Elkhart County Fair is a partnership between the Nappanee Noon Kiwanis and the Elkhart County Beef Cattle Association. The cattlemen provide the vision and the brand and the Kiwanis provide the management and the extra labor needed to grill and serve the thousands of sandwiches during the ten-day fair. The old timers still refer to the permanent building as a 'tent' because that is how it started.

Our county fair is one of the largest in the country and one of the top ticketed events in Indiana. The grandstand entertainment historically has the reputation of providing concerts that read like a who's-who in the world of music. The 'Ribeye Tent' has the honor of providing the fair food for the acts on Tuesday nights, before the show. The nights that I would volunteer, I made it a tradition to bring a few dozen ears of our Bullard Farms Sweet Corn to grill and enjoy with the other volunteers that evening.

Tuesday, July 27, 1993 was one of those nights. Johnny Cash and June Carter Cash were the entertainment that evening. I believe, past fair presidents and cattlemen, Denny Sharkey and Larry Struble delivered the Ribeye sandwiches that evening backstage and they took several ears of our corn along to the Cash family. The next day an article appeared in the South Bend Tribune where June Carter Cash was quoted as saying, "I'm busy, because my teeth is full of corn. Best corn in the whole world, and that's all I've got to say – except I'm glad to be here." South Bend Tribune 7-28-1993.

Our dogs...

I have had the pleasure of being in the company of dogs my entire life. It is impossible to write farm stories without stories about farm dogs. Our collie, Lassie, was our farm dog when I was young and I remember her being always present. Lassie was included in almost every family picture. Belle followed Lassie and she was more of a watchdog. She was always around the action on the farm. She was in the irrigation lanes, in the fields, or on guard around the farm. She was also collie. Belle had a different bark for different visitors or neighbors. She had a salesman bark, a school bus bark, a mailman bark, a Verlin (a neighbor) bark, a grandparent Bullard bark, a grandparent Beehler bark, and an unknown visitor bark. Belle only bit two people in her entire life, a father and son. 15 years elapsed between those two bites. She ended her long life by napping under the wheels of our grain truck and did not escape as the truck backed up. I hand painted her epitaph on a board that marked her grave. "Here lies a great dog. Belle."

Our family dogs started replacing the farm's dogs after Belle. In the fall of 1979, we had a large Angus production sale and my AGR pledge brother, Dale Grubbs, came up from his farm in southern Indiana to help with our sale. Grubbs Angus had a sale scheduled in late September and I went down to his farm to return the favor. On his sale day, there was someone that had a litter of Australian Shepard pups for sale. As pups will do, they were all jumping around their portable pen and smothered anyone that paid attention to them.

There was one female who just sat in the back watching the chaos. I paid the price of $75 and chose the obvious pup. We named her Cisco. She was, by instinct, a cattle dog. She knew where every cow was supposed to be and would rather ride in the bed of the truck than in the cab. At her athletic peak she could jump into the truck bed over the end gate. She knew voice and hand commands. I got into the habit of introducing the future farm dog as a pup to our aging, well-trained dog. The pup would learn fast from her mentor. Our next dog was a border collie pup from Bordner Angus Farms. Cisco had started to become less interested in farm duties. We named her Queenie. Beth and I joke that 'Queenie' raised our four children. Queenie was dialed in every minute. She would herd our kids, retrieve anything thrown, and guard the driveway with relentless energy. Queenie would use her intelligence and athleticism with intent. When people would pull into our drive to ask directions, ask for gas, or try to sell something, they would rarely exit their vehicle. They would ask, "Does she bite?" I would always reply, "I'm not sure" or "It depends."

I was in the back yard one day while the kids were playing in the treehouse, when a young man managed to make it to the door of our house to ask for gas. Beth answered the door, surprised that anyone would be able to ring the doorbell. Queenie positioned herself at the bottom of the steps. When Beth explained that we did not have any gas his tone changed to express disbelief. Queenie immediately sensed his change in attitude and proceeded to assert her authority and bit him as he left our property. A few hours later a sheriff's deputy showed up to file a report as the man had obviously filed a complaint. Beth had all of Queenie's shots up to date and the officer had no problem with her protecting our home.

When Queenie got older, we got a red heeler pup from a neighbor farmer and named her Lucy, after Lucille Ball and the television show, "I Love Lucy". She was in a difficult environment and I rescued her when she was only four weeks old. For several weeks, she resided in my Carhart jacket pocket when I was on the farm. Lucy was the easiest, smartest, 'large-and-in-charge' dog that I have ever known. Rats, mice, woodchucks, and disagreeable people were all on her endangered list. One disagreeable person teased her when she was a very small puppy. He was working on a scaffold as Lucy barked from below. I came into the space to witness the exchange and he asked me if his teasing pissed me off. I replied that "he wouldn't have to ask; he would know if I was pissed off." I fired him from the jobsite. Her record for woodchuck kills was 14 in one summer. Just a small amount of praise would encourage her to seek and destroy those vermin. Purdue University introduced woodchucks to Northern Indiana in the 1950's for the purpose of creating burrows for rabbits. The unintended consequence was the hundreds of millions of dollars of building damage and crop damage that they caused. One woodchuck den can destroy ¼ acre of soybeans.

Our phone rang one night, waking us at 2:30 a.m. A neighbor was calling me to ask for help. His cattle had broken out of their pen and they were wandering the fields and roads in the dark. I agreed to help and right before I hung up the phone, he added "Can you bring Lucy?" When I arrived at his farm, I joked that he mainly wanted her to come, not me. We drove back to where his Holstein steers were gathered along a fence row, and I let Lucy out of the truck bed. The cattle's attitude changed immediately and they headed back to their barn.

Part of the way back to the barn, as usually happens, one steer challenged her guidance and broke from the herd and took off running in the opposite direction. The farmer was worried but all I had to do was signal Lucy to go get him. We could not see her in the dark, but soon the steer came running back to join the small herd of escapees. The barn lot gate was open and soon the steers were all back home and counted.

The farmer apologized for the call and thanked me. I told him that the call could have been worse at 2:30 in the morning, as we had teenagers, aging parents, and cattle of our own. I had a toolbox fastened in the bed of my truck and it served as Lucy's favorite perch when the truck wasn't moving. She was with me when I dropped a donation at the local animal shelter and she jumped up on the toolbox to wait for my return. I rarely locked my truck when she was along, and sometimes even left it running if it was a quick trip.

Anyone that asked if they could pet her, I recommended against it because "she really likes her truck" and showed them my finger pretending that it was half-bitten off. While dropping off the donation a woman came into the shelter to chastise whomever had left the dog on a toolbox untethered. She was worried that Lucy would jump out or fall out and get hurt! I told her not to worry because Lucy was much smarter than any human. We buried Lucy by the fence at the entrance of the farm so that she could still stand guard. Lucy lived to be 17 years-old.

Lucy

I have already written some words about how our dog, Harley, got her name. Harley, our Aussiedoodle, never had the opportunity to be a true farm dog but she currently is in charge of security. Whether standing at the courtyard gate or at her spot at our bay window, she keeps us informed of everything that is going on in our neighborhood. I have never had a dog that truly worries about me like she does. I believe she knew of my cancer months before my diagnosis. She would not leave my side. She is able to smile, give me the 'side eye', and wins every stare down contest. Our non-farm dogs included Izzy, a rescued Westie. She had been abused and over-bred by a puppy mill. After being forced to whelp multiple litters a year, her teeth were falling out, her coat was sparce, and she was lice infested. She was under-weight and exhausted. Beth rescued her and nursed her back to health. Great food, vet care, grooming, vitamins, and love transformed Izzy into show-dog form. She was funny and energetic and lived out her life loved and happy. Daisy was a lab that we fostered as a service dog. She had been trained by incarcerated men and the foster program's purpose was to introduce her to kids, cats, TV, sofas, and all situations that she might encounter during her service duty. Our family met all of those requirements.

Daisy could ring a bell when she needed outside and responded to the word 'hurry' to do her duty. She could take the laundry out of the dryer and put it in a basket. We took her to movies, restaurants and shopping. She learned to accept kids, fish, cats, and other dogs. Beth and I even took her to a Purdue Basketball game at Mackey Arena, West Lafayette, Indiana. We contacted the arena staff to inquire about the protocol of bringing a service dog in training and they were 100% on board. When we got to our seats and got Daisy settled, all of our neighboring seatmates were appreciative except one woman. She was noticeably disagreeable and proceeded to report us to the ushers.

As the ushers came up the steps to where we were seated, we were uncertain about what was going to happen. They motioned for us to come with them and they took us to the best seats in Mackey. Everything that happens in Mackey is great! Beth also applied to adopt a retired greyhound. We had a local chapter that placed the racing dogs into adoptive homes and soon Cody was part of our household.

Most greyhounds are euthanized when they finish their racing careers or they are unable to win. Cody was four years old when we adopted him and we assumed he had done some winning. We had a big back yard and he frequently exhibited his speed. He was the king of zoomies. Cody taught me how to turn off the switch and instantly relax. He would come into the house after racing in the backyard and be asleep in minutes. I began to notice an unusual part of his daily routine. When Beth was away from the house he would wake from a deep sleep and walk over to our picture window and look outside. Several minutes later Beth would arrive at our home, pulling into the driveway. After a few times witnessing this behavior, I started to take more notes. This phenomenon would occur at different times of the day and Beth could arrive from any direction. I do not know how he knew of her pending arrival but I do know that he knew. We have much to learn.

Stella; Stella was our Newfoundland and her coat was black as night. She was, what I would describe, a gentle, comfortable dog. In line with her breed, she loved people and water in any form. She would lay in a kiddy pool, enjoy a sprinkler, or cool off in Lake Wawasee or Pine Creek. She had a special bond with our Westie, Zeno. She allowed him free reign to chew, kiss, gently bite, and love on her. She sadly contracted cancer and lived only a few years.

A few years after Stella was gone, we were on vacation in Sea Pines, South Carolina, with the dogs. In the fall, the community allows dogs to be off leash on the beach. I had taken the dogs for a walk on the beach in the morning and about 1/8 of a mile ahead on the beach, a family was playing with their dog, a black Newfie. Once Zeno spotted the dog, he tore off down the beach, certain that it was his long, lost friend, Stella. When he got about 10 feet from the dog, he stopped dead in his tracks, realizing it was not Stella.

The two dogs greeted each other and went on with their walks. I do not believe in coincidences, I will not forget this sad and joyful encounter. We have a lot to learn from dogs. The before-mentioned Zeno was our second Westie. Beth rescued him from a breeder who lived in our same town. His purpose was to be a stud that would produce show dogs. Zeno had just a little skip in his get-a-long when he ran and the breeder decided to sell him.

When we arrived, we found Zeno chained to a small wooden shelter. The connection between Beth and Zeno was immediate. The asking price was substantial and I put on my negotiator hat to haggle. They were hoping to build a kennel and I convinced them they needed a large stack of red tiles and several chain-link panels were known to me. The end result was rescuing Zeno to our care at a reasonable price. He has slowed recently, a little less tolerant, struggles with hearing and sight but he enjoys his walks, travel, and naps. We are happy that he is still with us and has earned the title, 'Old Man'. Long live Zeno!

Cleo was a German Shepherd mix and named after a famous psychic. Cleo was not as much a family dog, as she was our son, Peter's dog. Peter never was attached to our family's birds, fish, hamsters, dogs, cats, goats, chickens, etc., etc., etc. He was along with Beth grocery shopping and the store was having a 'pet adoption day'. Peter and Cleo locked eyes and it was over. Somehow, my approval was deemed warranted in this one case, and Pete was waiting for me when I got home. He had the money ready for the adoption and we went to the Humane Shelter and adopted Cleo. She soon became the perfect dog. She lived for the minute that Peter would get home from school. She was always ready to wrestle with any, and all, of our other dogs and she had moves that would make any NFL linebacker jealous. Their separation during Peter's first year at Purdue was hard on Cleo as well as Peter. She applied and was accepted to Purdue the following year. She became a fixture in the neighborhood where Peter lived in West Lafayette.

After graduation she traveled to Colorado with Peter where she lived out her life, happy and loved. Jordan...On the way to Bethany School to pick up our son, Alex, Beth noticed a sign next to a long driveway that stated, 'puppies for sale'. The magnetic pull of this sign was powerful. Beth and Alex picked a puppy out of the Jack Russel/Fox Terrier mix litter. Dogs, especially puppies, complete life. We were in the middle of produce season and Beth gathered a group of workers and our kids for reinforcement, as she brought the tiny puppy to me for the introduction. Beth was well prepared for my reaction as she held out the palm-sized puppy. "We named him Jordan," after 'Michael Jordan'. Well-played, Beth, well-played.

As a small puppy, Jordan would sit patiently by the door to be let out. He was very smart and obedient. I believe if I would have called him to jump off a cliff he would have obeyed. A friend to all, RIP Jordan. Murphy, the 'Desert Dog', was another one of our rescues. He chose Beth at a vendor event. A small white dog mix, he was advertised as being two years old. I aged him at 10. He was funny and loved life as soon as we got him healthy. He was part of our pack as we traveled in our small RV. It was at Joshua Tree National Park where he earned his nickname, Desert Dog.

We tethered the dogs as we set up our camping spot and kept a close eye on the dogs as it was 99 degrees. We called them into the camper for an AC and water break but Murphy was not responding to our calls. We found him comfortably laying behind the camper, in the sun, smiling ear to ear. His nickname, Desert Dog, was born. On our trip to Acadia National Park, Murphy experienced a mini-stroke and kept circling rather than walking. We weighed several options just in case he passed on the trip. In a few days he snapped out of the symptoms. He lived long enough to make the move to Phoenix and was rewarded by being buried in the desert when he passed.

Ella...Beth's shadow. Ella, short for Cinderella, is a goldendoodle with the coloring classified as "mackerel" which is a mottled black and grey. She is caring and comfortable. A 'happy-go-lucky' description has been used by her trainer and groomer. She loves to kiss ears and necks and will hug anyone. She carries on conversations with neighborhood dogs across our walls and is constantly on high alert for anything that moves or has been moved. She is concerned when Beth is out of her sight and waits patiently for her return. She visits my lap during these waits for assurance of Beth's return. If dogs could outlive us, Ella would be an easy choice. The rest...Beth and I have always agreed to have four dogs. Freud might diagnose us as needing a substitute for our four kids, or it might be that we are able to manage.

Perky, Mickey, Asher, Lilley, Kashi, and Naki were also part of our clan. RBGB, Ruth Bader Ginsburg Bullard, was added to our pack during this edit. Ruthie is a silky wired-haired dachshund. We are back up to four dogs.

Art and Jo Lockwood...

Art and Jo lived across the street from the farm. Art was a retired railroad engineer and almost aways wore a striped blue and grey railroad hat. He knew how to braid rope and filet fish to perfection.

Art and Jo would keep watch on our farm and I would categorize them as perfect neighbors. When we started selling sweet corn on the corner, Art would come down and share stories and help sort and sell. He taught me, by example, how to deal with the rare complaints. He knew how to present the produce and was friendly and courteous to everyone. The following thoughts were written by me in our farm office on the morning that I heard of his passing.

"As the birds chirp, the wind drifts, and a perfect summer morning is gone... Art Lockwood has passed with the morning. The kids are at the fair, the irrigation sprinklers are running, and the sweet corn, that Art loved to sell, is growing.

Art was with us from the start and he would be quick to tell you that, 'anyone could sell this corn'. Art was a prince of a guy and I will think of him every time someone wants a half dozen." Some of his knowledge and advice follow.

"Some of the best we've ever raised"

"My personal favorite is yellow, but I like my corn yellow and my tomatoes red"

"I am glad you told me, that way we can make it right"

"Kurt, pick this young lady out a good cantaloupe"

"Too bad they don't have zippers on those melons"

"we'll make out O.K."

Art was a life coach and I miss him.

Dwight Fish...

I met Dwight at an Elkhart County Democratic monthly meeting in 2008 and he quickly became a good friend. In 2008, the entire sane world was ready to move on from Bush's failed policies. Dwight had worked on his neighbor's farms growing up and he wanted to come out and see our farm. Dwight soon became a valued part of our farm operation. He enjoyed driving tractor, he helped with irrigation, drove truck during harvest, and helped bale hay. He drove the IH 68 Superhayliner baler behind our 7110 Case tractor.

My first pick of baling jobs was to stack the wagon, so this arrangement worked out nicely. He refused any payment for his labor, as instructed by his wife, Oxana. We perfected our use of the barter system. He currently is an Elkhart City Councilman. Dwight volunteers a great deal of his time at his church, the Art League, and the Railroad museum in Elkhart. His friendship is a valuable part of my life.

Steve Rumfelt...

Steve owned a welding shop about a mile and a half west of our farm, called Intruder Products. For many years we used A and R welding shop in Middlebury for farm repairs and fabrication of inventions. I think I met Steve during a random stop at his shop inquiring about a welding job we needed done. His quality of work and location of his shop led us to use him almost exclusively for our welding. Steve could weld anything metal.

He was the guy that everyone called or referred when the job was labeled 'impossible' by mere mortal welders. They would say, "It can't be done, but I know a guy!" Welding on the Alaskan pipeline, nuclear power plants, the Lilypads at the Wellfield Botanical Garden in Elkhart, the bomb explosion container for the local police department and repairing the brass railing at the Lerner Theatre in Elkhart were just a few of the jobs on his long resume. He was forgiving and giving to a fault. He refused to teach me how to weld because he thought I would no longer need his abilities.

We traded work and there were only a few times that I forced him to take payment. We agreed that if he was happy and I was happy, no one else should care. We moved buildings to different towns, a gazebo across town, a printing press, disabled vehicles, and semi-trailers.

He repaired irrigation pipes and pumps while they were under pressure for me, as well as tractors, implements, and my John Deere 7700 combine. We own a Pettibone Army forklift together, that we named the 'Big Machine', along with Steve Vlaeminck. I love to drive it. Steve's brother, Bob bought it from an army surplus in Iowa. It could lift 70,000 pounds, pull 1,000,000 pounds.

It originally was used to clear wreckage from aircraft carrier decks. When I would use it to pile silage onto a stack, Dad and Steve were always worried I would roll it off the stack. We used to move small buildings, grain bins, semi-trailers and load equipment on to trailers. I used it break up concrete, demo buildings, and dig up buried tanks.

Steve and I are no longer farming or welding in his shop but I can still smell the wood burning in his shop stove, feel the oily surface of new steel, see the flash of the welding rods, dodge the sparks and hear the whine of the grinders, and I can still see his blueprints that he drew on a Mayberry Café napkin in my memories.

The 'Big Machine'

Beth...the Story of Us.

Beth and I met the first time when we were freshman at Purdue University. We were getting a ride home with a mutual friend. Kurt Laidig and Beth had both attended Penn High School and Kurt and I both lived in Wiley Hall and our fathers knew each other. He had played football and basketball and she was a Pennette and active in many school programs. I sat in the back of his car and listened to their high school stories. I was tiny and she was uninterested and I thought she was way out of my league. Fast forward five years. We were both out of college, I was working on the farm and she was working for Boise

Cascade in LaPorte and living in South Bend.

I had grown 8" taller and had gained 60 pounds of muscle. I had heard she was in the area from a fraternity brother. It was the mid-70s, and dancing in clubs was the normal nightly activity. At the Moonraker nightclub, on ladies' night, I recognized her and asked her to dance. Our first song was 'Shadow Dancing' by Andy Gibb.

There were at least 10 clubs in the area where you could dance and hitting 3 or 4 clubs a night was not uncommon. She had no idea who I was and I asked if her name was Beth Carpenter. She said, "no, its Carmichael". We were married eleven months later. She still laughs at my jokes, and we both receive grief for striving to 'do the right thing'. She is smart, possesses integrity, she is honest, and always presents herself in an attractive manner. She stayed home during our children's young years and her sacrifice is greatly under appreciated. Our country punishes stay-at-home parents for their entire lives. Society ignores the social and monetary contributions that stay-at-home parents make for their families and society as a whole. Their social security amounts are frozen in place simply by their decision to stay at home and raise their children.

We were fortunate to be able to provide adventures for our family, including Mackinaw Island, MI, Charleston and Hilton Head Island, SC, Mammoth Cave, KY, Disney World, Fort Wilderness, Universal Studios, Everglades Alligator Alley, Key West and Key Largo in Flori-da. We visited many County and State Parks, Chicago, and visits to Beth's mom in Florida. Farming and teaching allowed us time to enjoy these trips. Our family dynamic during these adventures could provide many yet-to-be-written sitcoms.

Beth and I have, almost always, been 'on the same page' presenting a united front in the war between parents and children. When difficult times surfaced it was usually money related. I believe Beth would have succeeded in any career and I felt sometimes that her being married to a 'farmer' prevented her from being included in Elkhart's inner circle. Their loss. I can't imagine any other person that would have been as accepting and more supportive of my life journey. My whitewater rafting trips, hiking, obsessions with basketball and the Glacier National Park, my wandering on our tours of Europe, my being the last on planes and boats, my positions on countless committees and boards have all been tolerated. I have jumped into many projects and business ventures and learned along the way.

My self-confidence was the perfect counterbalance to her doubt. We trust each other. Beth's intuition about situations and people is next level. It has proven true, time and time again. I am still learning how to immediately accept her assessment.

Another one of her life's achievements is her success of breaking the generational chain of bitterness and selfishness. She replaced those character traits with kindness and selflessness. As our lives progressed, we kept moving into older and older homes. She commented, "I don't think this is how it is supposed to work." We have lived in homes that were 100, 50, 90, and 130 years-old. We currently live in our newest home which is 40 years old. We have been traveling and enjoying retirement.

When we find ourselves experiencing a twinge of guilt, we remind each other of our decades of work and our sacrifices for others. The support and companionship of a life partner is priceless. I am lucky, proud, and grateful for Beth. May 19, 2026 will be 47 years of marriage for us. We have a 'Mighty Love'.

Beth and Kurt Bullard

The Decision to Sell the Farm...

Dad told me, from the time that I was young, that I would most likely be the one to 'pull the plug' and sell the farm. We sold the farm in August, 2021. Over his life, Dad witnessed the City of Elkhart moving east. He could see the future. He knew that someday it would be impossible to farm with the traffic and pressures of expanding development. The land values kept increasing, but no one could have imagined the value explosion caused by the frantic RV expansion during COVID. Everyone seemed to want an RV and the construction of new RV plants was on a fast track. Everything in life is about timing. Farming had become less enjoyable for me after Dad had passed. Beth was ready for ten years before I was ready to sell. I am uncertain of the exact day, or if anything of consequence happened that day, but I walked into the farmhouse kitchen through the back door and said to her, "I'm done." My corn crop was excellent and the price was at a record high. My hay crop was also excellent and the price was high.

COVID and the supply chain disruptions also produced record prices for used machinery. One of Dad's sayings was, "Don't let the watermelon get too ripe!" For many years, modern day carpetbaggers, (and/or vultures), would drive into our farm offering to buy our land. We had sold some land in the past, but every time it was by necessity, for the survival of the farm. A trapped animal will chew it's leg off to escape the trap. This is the metaphor I would use when nosy neighbors would question our decision to sell part of the farm. They were disappointed in our decision to sell even part of our farm because it provided them with hunting, hiking, fuel for their fireplaces, and scenic views. Beth and I decided to send inquiry letters to surrounding businesses, offering our land to them if, by chance, they wanted to expand their current operations. Almost all of these businesses were located on land that we once owned or farmed. We received some interest but most balked at our asking price. An RV building spree took place during COVID and the price of land soon eclipsed our asking price from just a few years earlier. A developer, needing land inventory, got our attention with a valid offer.

At the same time one of my previous contacts became interested as well. The developer and his agent wanted almost immediate possession because they "didn't want an old farmhouse in front of their new beautiful factory." This rude comment made me thankful that Beth had left her 'light saber' at home. The back-and-forth bidding between potential buyers awarded the sale to an investor group from Mishawaka. They had no agenda and no moving deadline for us to honor. They allowed us time to sell all of the equipment and farm materials, find a home, and move. The farmstead had 15 buildings full of 130 years of accumulation. We held the farm's very first auction, we had a moving sale, and I took equipment to two Brightstar farm auctions at their sale location in Middlebury, IN. We gave tools and tractors to friends and family. We also had a constant pile of 'free' items out by the road. We were able to donate historical items to nine museums and non-profits. It was cathartic to sort through all of the treasures and memories. Certain people might have thought the items were 'mostly junk', but I have always appreciated the farm's history and the stories those items held. Our farm was over half the age of the country.

I was unsuccessful in getting our farm office donated to Krider Nursery and World's Fair Garden in Middlebury. Dad had purchased the small building at an auction in the 1960s. There was a group of these small cabins along SR 120 between Bristol and Howe, Indiana. They were used as sleeping cabins for travelers during the 1933 World's Fair in Chicago. Before the interstate highway system was built in the 50's, travelers would use SR 120, US 33, US20, and US 12 to travel the east/west route. The overnight fee was $2.50.

There were also sleeping cabins along SR 120 west of Bristol and a few sleeping cabins in Benton along US 33. I followed a lead to disassemble our main barn and have it moved to Alaska but that also proved unsuccessful. Our double corn crib, was a Purdue University design, and I hoped it would be accepted by a farm museum in Atlanta, IN. That also did not bear fruit. I was the first and last to farm some of our family's land.

A worrisome calculation that I made during the decision process revealed the fact that our selling price was more per acre than the accumulated gross farming receipts over the 130-year time span of our family's ownership. The disappearance of farmland has two causes. The greed and profit potential of industry and commercial property is too great and the profit realized from farming is too small. It took us an entire year to disperse our farm's accumulation and find a home. We relocated to Phoenix, Arizona where our daughter, Morgan, and her family live. We live there today.

Epilogue

Without a doubt, there are many stories that I have left out of this book. I have tried to include stories that are positive, educational, and humorous. These are stories that have made an impact on my life. When my Dad got 'up in age', I was driving with him in his truck headed to the Centreville Fair, when he calmly said, "There's a nice tree." I would expect that sense of wonder from a toddler, who might be seeing something for the first time, but not from my fearless, strong, bib-overall wearing father. I understand it now. Not only was he in awe of seeing that particular tree for the first time, but he had come to the realization that it might be the last time.

If you have lost your sense of wonder due to a loss or a health crisis, or just because you are 'getting up in age', I urge you to reignite. Even if it is noticing a nice tree. If you have been made aware of this book and were able to read it all of the way to the end, thank-you. If you have a memory of our farm that you would like to share, please contact me at kurtbullard4444@gmail.com. I cannot guarantee a second book, but it should be easier the second time around. A neighbor farmer, Fred Eby, said, "the advantage of making mistakes, is that you shouldn't make them a second time." Fred was born in 1875 and his words are still true. I have a title 'penciled in' for the second attempt and a few stories already jotted down. 'Beyond the Two Miles' will include problems, hurdles, hoops, mistakes, and more lessons. Thanks again for reading 'Bullard Road'.

Acknowledgements

I would like to thank Beth and our children for keeping me grounded. I would also like to thank 'As You Wish Publishing' for helping me 'storm the castle'. Additional thanks go to Beth for helping me edit the book and choose words. Thanks to my Mom for passing her fearlessness to me. I would also like to thank Shana Dines, local artist and author, for her friendship and inspiration to write. Thank you to my grandson, Hudson Vanderwall, for his expertise in increasing the resolution of my old photos. Thanks to my sister, Michelle, for being a reliable family resource. Thanks to everyone that participated in making these stories possible. "Memories are treasures time cannot destroy, The happy pathways to Yesterday's joy". (Unknown greeting card that Mom quoted.)

About The Author

Kurt is in a unique position to tell these stories. He has been a life-long farmer and the fifth generation Bullard to live and work on the original farmstead. Kurt is a storyteller, a joke teller, risk taker and problem solver. Many of the people that he has written about have helped shape his character. He still plays basketball, enjoys collecting antiques, paddleboarding the Salt River, Arizona, and traveling the world with his wife, Beth. He is one of the founding members of the Elkhart County Beef Cattle Association and co-founded Seed to Feed, which is a non-profit that grows fresh produce for food pantries. Kurt has been the co-chair of his Concord High School reunion committee for over 50 years. He graduated from Purdue University in 1975 with an Agronomy degree and is a member of Alpha Gamma Rho fraternity. He has used his experience to help fund many projects and has served and presided over many boards and committees. Kurt is still an active participant in building community and preserving history.

www.ingramcontent.com/pod-product-compliance
Lightning Source LLC
Chambersburg PA
CBHW051806050726
47598CB00006B/2445